Kids can Knit

Kids can Knit

Fun and easy projects
for small knitters

Carolyn Clewer

A QUARTO BOOK

Published in 2004 by Silverdale Books
An imprint of Bookmart Ltd
Registered Number 2372865
Trading as Bookmart Limited
Blaby Road
Wigston
Leicester LE18 4SE

ISBN 1-84509-096-9

QUAR: KFK

Conceived, designed and produced by
Quarto Publishing plc
The Old Brewery
6 Blundell Street
London N7 9BH

Project editor: Michelle Pickering
Art editor: Anna Knight
Assistant art director: Penny Cobb
Copy editor: Claire Waite-Brown
Pattern checker: Pauline Hornsby
Designer: Caroline Grimshaw
Illustrator: Coral Mula
Photographers: Paul Forrester and
Colin Bowling
Indexer: Madaleine Combie
Art director: Moira Clinch
Publisher: Piers Spence

Manufactured by Universal Graphics Pte
Ltd, Singapore
Printed by Star Standard Industries (Pte)
Ltd, Singapore

Yarn quantities

The projects in this book give the quantity of yarn by length. This is the
safest way because different brands of yarn can vary quite a lot – a 50g
(1¾oz) ball of yarn from one manufacturer might contain fewer
metres or yards than the same type of yarn from another
manufacturer, even though they both weigh the same. If you buy
the correct length, you will always have enough to finish the project.
As a rough guide, however, 50g (1¾oz) of cotton double-knitting = 85m
(95yds); 50g (1¾oz) acrylic/wool double-knitting = 120m (135yds);
50g (1¾oz) Aran = 80m (90yds); 50g (1¾oz) mohair = 100m (110yds);
50g (1¾oz) chunky = 50m (55yds); 50g (1¾oz) super chunky = 40m
(45yds) ; and 25g (1oz) glittery crochet thread = 100m (110yds).

Needle sizes

All of the needle sizes in this book are given in modern metric
measurements. In the past, different measurement systems were used,
called imperial and American. So, if you borrow or buy old knitting
needles, here's how to convert them to metric sizes:

Metric	Imperial	American	Metric	Imperial	American
2mm	14	0	5.5mm	5	9
2.25mm	13	1	6mm	4	10
2.75mm	12	2	6.5mm	3	10½
3mm	11	3	7mm	2	10½
3.25mm	10	4	7.5mm	1	11
3.75mm	9	5	8mm	0	11
4mm	8	6	9mm	00	13
4.5mm	7	7	10mm	000	15
5mm	6	8			

Contents

Introduction

Knitting is a way of making a stretchy fabric from a long length of yarn. For hundreds of years, all sorts of people have knitted all kinds of things, all over the world. You can knit crazy and original things as well as useful and practical ones. Once you have started to knit, you will discover a fun and creative hobby to continue for the rest of your life.

Hand knitting

When you look at a sweater or a woolly scarf, you can clearly see if it has been knitted. The knitting in this book is hand knitting, which is simple to learn and fun to do. Sometimes things are knitted by machine, which is faster. The stitches can be much finer, but they are still made in the same way. Some T-shirts, socks and even dishcloths are machine knitted. The projects in this book teach you how to hand knit. You will find out how to use the basic equipment and materials and, by following step-by-step instructions and colourful illustrations, you will master simple techniques to make 16 lively projects.

Learning step by step

Every time a new skill is introduced, there is a project that you can follow to practise it. Starting with finger knitting, you can have fun using colourful yarns, and you will soon discover how easy it is to cast on and knit with needles. You will learn simple knitting techniques while making exciting items for yourself and for friends. You will enjoy picking up new skills, like shaping, while knitting fried eggs, and trying out purl stitch on a string of silly sausages. After these projects you will find instructions for making garments that you can wear, like a poncho, a Peruvian hat and a striped sweater. If you run out of yarn and want to keep knitting, there's even a chapter that offers ideas for how to make your own yarn.

Playing with yarn

Before you start to knit, it's a good idea to experiment with a few different types of yarn to see how they look and feel. The easiest and most enjoyable way to do this is by learning some basic knitting skills that don't require needles. The simplest sort of knitting is finger knitting. It is really easy to do and you can use any yarn you can find. It will also help you to learn how a knitted stitch is formed out of a loop of yarn. In this chapter you will also find out how to make a tube of knitting using a spool knitter, and how to make fluffy pompoms and braids.

Finger knitting

Finger knitting is an easy way of knitting a chain of yarn without using knitting needles. Double-knitting or chunky yarn is easy to use when learning new techniques, but you can try finger knitting with any yarn.

When we refer to the 'working end' of the yarn, this simply means the end that comes from the ball. The loose end is therefore the other end.

1 Tie the loose end of the yarn around your index finger. Hold your hand with your palm facing you. Keep the loose end of the yarn against your palm and hold the working end in your other hand.

2 Wrap the working end of the yarn once around your index finger, ending just above the knot. You now have two loops around your finger.

3 Let go of the working end and use your fingers to lift the bottom loop up over the top loop.

4 Drop this loop off the end of your finger, leaving just one loop on your finger once again.

5 Now wrap the working end of the yarn around your finger above the loop. Lift the bottom loop over the top loop and drop it, just like you did before in Steps 3–4.

6 Follow Steps 3–5 to continue making the chain in the same way. You can make the chain as long as you want, or just keep practising until you get the hang of it.

7 To finish, cut the working end of the yarn about 10cm (4in) from the end of the chain. Gently slide your finger out of the last loop. Thread the cut end of the yarn through the loop and pull tightly to seal the chain.

Materials

- About 100m (110yds) of yarn

- Spool knitter

- Tapestry needle

- Scissors

- Beads, buttons or sew-on toy eyes

- Cardboard

- Four dishes or jars of different diameters to draw around to make circles for pompom making. Their diameters should be approximately 15cm (6in), 8cm (3in), 5cm (2in) and 3cm (1in)

- Tapestry needle

Making the body

▲ Make a big pompom for the spider's body.

1 A giant pompom is going to be the body of the spider. Cut out two cardboard discs, each with a 15cm (6in) outer circle and a 5cm (2in) central hole. This will make a nice, fat body for your spider.

2 Wind the yarn around the discs until there is still just enough room to push your finger through the hole in the middle. You could try making a patterned pompom by winding layers of different coloured yarns around the discs. Don't cut or tie the pompom yet.

Furry fun!

Assembling the pieces

▲ Thread the spool-knitted legs through the hole in the pompom.

1 Thread the four lengths of spool knitting that you made for the spider's legs exactly halfway through the hole in the middle of the pompom.

▲ Cut around the cardboard discs.

2 Now carefully cut around the pompom, between the discs. Don't cut the legs.

▲ Tie some strong yarn tightly around the middle of the pompom.

3 Use a strong yarn to tie the pompom securely, trapping the legs into place. Do not trim the ends yet.

▲ Tie the finger-knitted dangling string around the middle of the pompom.

4 Now tie one end of the finger knitting tightly around the middle of the pompom to fix the dangling string in place.

5 Now you can remove the cardboard discs from the pompom.

Making the head

1 Make a smaller pompom for the spider's head, this time using 8cm (3in) discs with 3cm (1in) holes.

▲ Remove the cardboard discs but don't trim the ties.

2 Cut and tie the pompom with a length of strong yarn and remove the discs. Do not trim the ties yet.

Attaching the head

▲ Knot the ties together to join the two pompoms.

1 Join the head and body by knotting together the ties on both pompoms as tightly as you can.

2 Trim the loose ends and, hey presto, your spider has a head.

Adding eyes

▲ Stitch some eyes onto the spider's head.

1 Dangle your spider to check how it will hang. Using a tapestry needle, stitch two beads, buttons or sew-on toy eyes into place. Stitch firmly through the middle of the head so that the eyes are held securely.

Now find a cat or other friend – they don't have to be furry! – and start dangling.

Pick up your needles

Now it's time to knit with two needles. In this chapter you will learn how to cast on stitches, how to knit using the basic knit stitch and how to cast off when you have finished a piece of knitting. All knitting is based on these important skills. The projects that follow the techniques will help you to put your newly learned knitting skills into practice, so what are you waiting for? Pick up your needles and start knitting.

Casting on

Casting on is the process of making your first row of stitches on a knitting needle. There are several different ways of casting on, but making a slipknot is always the first step.

Remember that the working end of the yarn comes from the ball, so the loose end is, of course, the other end.

Making a slipknot

1 Grip the loose end of the yarn between your thumb and hand with your palm facing towards you.

3 Using the finger and thumb of your other hand, reach down into the loop that you have made and pull through the working end of the yarn to form a new loop.

2 Wrap the working end of the yarn right around your first two fingers.

4 Hold this loop with one hand and pull the loose end of the yarn with the other hand. Simple.

You have now made a slipknot.

Simple cast-on

1 Slide the slipknot onto the knitting needle and gently tighten it. This forms your first stitch.

2 Hold the needle in one hand and grip the working end of the yarn with the fingers of your other hand.

3 Wrap the working end of the yarn around your thumb so that it forms a loop.

All of the projects in this book tell you exactly how many stitches to cast on, but right now you just need to do about 10 to 20 stitches to practise the techniques.

4 Push the tip of the needle up through the loop on your thumb.

5 Slip your thumb out of the loop and gently pull the working end of the yarn to tighten the new stitch on the needle.

6 Repeat Steps 3–5 until you have around 10 or 20 stitches on the needle, depending on how much practice you want to do.

Tip

When tightening the stitches, make sure that they are still loose enough to slide up and down the needle easily.

Holding the needles and yarn

So far you have worked with only a single needle. To start knitting, you will need to get used to holding two needles and the yarn all at the same time. Just like anything new, it will feel a bit strange at first, but with a bit of practice you will soon get used to it. Cast on about 10 to 20 stitches and you are ready to start.

Holding the needles

When you are about to start knitting, hold the needle with the cast-on stitches in your left hand and hold the empty needle in your right hand.

1 Hold your left hand lightly over the top of the needle, gripping the tip of the needle between your thumb and index finger.

3 Now try holding the empty needle in your right hand like a knife, with your hand over the top of the needle. You can tuck the end of the needle under your arm if your needles are long enough to do this.

2 Take the empty needle in your right hand, holding it like a pencil. The needle should rest on top of your hand between the thumb and index finger.

Sewing in loose ends

1 When the needles are no longer in the knitting, you will be left with two loose strands of yarn, one at each end of the knitting. Thread the loose strand at the cast-off edge onto a tapestry needle.

2 On the wrong side of the knitting, stitch under and over the nearest six or seven stitches, following the row along the cast-off edge of the knitting.

3 Stretch the knitting a bit to loosen the woven-in end so that it is not too tight.

5 Trim the yarn, leaving a short tail showing on the wrong side.

6 Repeat Steps 1–5 with the loose strand at the cast-on edge.

7 If you are knitting something big, you will usually have to use more than one ball of yarn (you'll learn how to do this on page 48). Wherever you've started a new ball, you'll be left with two loose ends of yarn at the edge of your knitting. Sew these into your knitting in the same way as before, but follow the vertical edge of the knitting instead of working along a row.

4 Double back, stitching back into the woven-in yarn to make the end really secure.

Can you believe how easy it is to knit? Well, let's start using your new skill to make some fun and useful things.

Funny-face bag

This drawstring bag is easy to make. It's a great way of using up odd balls of yarn and will give you a chance to practise casting on, doing the knit stitch and casting off. Then you can decorate the bag with stitching, embroidery and fringing.

If you follow the instructions here, you will make a small bag that can be used as a treasure pouch or purse and doesn't take long to make. If you want to make a bigger bag, you can keep knitting until you've had enough, or until you run out of yarn. The longer you knit, the longer your bag will be. Have fun making a quirky face by adding eyes, a nose, a mouth and hair. Silly, cute or ugly, you can't go wrong! You could even try making a whole crazy bag family in different sizes.

You are now going to use the knitting skills you learned on pages 24–31. If you need a reminder of how to do something, just look back to the pictures and instructions there.

Let's get knitting!

Knitting the bag

1 Cast on 30 stitches using the simple cast-on method and double-knitting yarn.

▲ Knit the bag using the knit stitch.

2 Knit each stitch on every row until your piece of knitting is about 30cm (12in) long.

3 Cast off and sew in the loose ends of yarn at the cast-off and cast-on edges.

▲ The funny face needs to fit onto one half of the knitting.

4 Fold the knitting in half to find the bottom edge of the bag (this is shown by a dotted line in the picture). Remember that the face needs to fit onto the front of the bag, so think about where you want to position the eyes, nose and mouth.

5 Use a tapestry needle and oddments of yarn to sew on a pair of toy eyes or buttons.

Materials

- About 100m (110yds) of double-knitting or Aran yarn for the bag
- Assorted oddments of yarn for the face, hair and seams
- 4mm knitting needles
- Scissors
- Tapestry needle
- Toy eyes or buttons
- Length of narrow ribbon, spool knitting or braid
- Crochet hook
- Tapestry needle

Chain-stitch mouth

1 You are now going to use chain stitch and an oddment of yarn to make a smiley mouth. Put a knot in the end of the yarn and thread the other end through a tapestry needle.

2 Start sewing by pushing the needle through the knitting from the wrong side. The side where you've sewn the eyes will be the right side of the bag, so the other side is therefore the wrong side.

▲ Push the needle back through to the wrong side, leaving a small loop.

3 Push the needle back through the knitting in almost the same place, leaving a loop of thread sticking out.

▲ Bring the needle up through the loop to make the first chain stitch.

4 Move the needle along a little to begin the next stitch. Pass the needle through to the front of your knitting, coming up inside the loop you just made. Then push the needle down again through the same place, creating a new loop as you go.

▲ Keep sewing chain stitches to make the mouth.

5 Keep making loopy stitches by repeating Steps 2–4 and you will soon see a 'chain' of stitching appear. Give him a nice big grin.

Satin-stitch nose

1 Satin stitch is a different type of stitch that you can use to make a round nose as big or as small as you like. Knot the end of another oddment of yarn and thread the other end through the tapestry needle.

2 Pass the needle through the knitting from the wrong side, then pass it back through the knitting a little farther along to make a small stitch.

3 Now make another slightly bigger stitch just above the first.

▲ Use satin stitch to give your bag a nose.

4 Repeat Steps 2–3, making bigger and then smaller stitches until you have made a round nose just the size that you want. Not only can you knit, but now you know two embroidery stitches as well.

Fringe hair

1 To make a woolly fringe for the hair, cut several pieces of yarn about 15cm (6in) long. Thick or fluffy yarn will work well.

2 Take two or more pieces and fold them in half to make a loop.

▲ Use a crochet hook to pull a loop of yarn through the edge of the bag.

3 At the cast-on edge of the knitting, starting on one side, push a crochet hook from the wrong side to the right side (the front of the bag). Use the hook to pull the loop of yarn through from the right side to the wrong side.

▲ Pull the ends of the piece of fringe through the loop.

4 Now use the crochet hook to pull the ends of the yarn through the loop.

▲ Tighten the knot to make the fringe stick out from the top of the bag.

5 Pull the yarn to tighten the knot so that the loose ends stick out like hair.

6 Repeat Steps 2–5 until the cast-on edge is covered in fringe, then do the same thing all along the cast-off edge.

Oversewing the seams

1 Fold the bag in half so that the side seams meet exactly and you can see the face you have made.

2 Thread a tapestry needle with a yarn that contrasts in colour to the knitting, so that it will stand out. Knot one end of the yarn.

▲ Keeping the knot inside the bag, push the needle through to the front.

3 The oversewing method is an easy and decorative way to sew seams. Starting at the bottom corner, make sure that the knot is on the inside of the bag, and stitch through to the front of the knitting.

▲ Use oversewing stitch to sew the seam of your bag.

4 Take the yarn over the edge to the back of the bag, a bit farther along, and stitch through both layers to the front. Work along the seam in this way until you get to the top.

▲ Make the seam secure by sewing a double stitch at the end.

5 Do a double stitch at the end to keep the seam from coming undone. Pass the needle through to the inside of the bag and cut the yarn.

6 Now repeat Steps 2–5 on the other side of the bag.

Drawstring

▲ Thread a drawstring around the top of the bag.

1 You can make a drawstring using a length of narrow ribbon, spool knitting or braid. Using a crochet hook or your fingers, thread the drawstring in and out of the knitted stitches around the top of the bag.

2 Knot the ends of the drawstring, pull tight and your stuff will be safe!

Now that you've made a funny-face bag, why not make one for your best friend in different colours and with an even funnier face?

Rainbow friendship bands

Choose a rainbow of your best friend's favourite colours to create this striped bracelet and choker. They are so pretty that you will want to make a set for yourself. You could even try making a matching flower, using the instructions for any of the Fantastic Flowers on pages 42–47, to decorate a special choker.

If you need help with some of the knitting skills used in this project, simply look back to pages 24–31, where all the techniques you will be using are explained.

Striped strands!

Seven-stripe bracelet

Arranging the stripes

Try different colour combinations until you find one you like.

1 Spend a little time before you start knitting on deciding which colours look best together. Lay out strands of yarn to make the best stripe pattern that you can. The final colour will need to be 1.5m (5ft) long and the other colours each need to be 1m (3ft) long.

Knitting the bracelet

1 Take the first 1m (3ft) length of yarn and make the cast-on slipknot about 20cm (8in) from the beginning of the strand. Cast on 24 stitches using the simple cast-on method.

Tie the second strand around the first strand at the beginning of the next row.

2 Now take the second coloured strand and tie it in a knot around the first strand of yarn, leaving an 20cm (8in) tail before the knot.

3 Slide the knot right up towards the first stitch of the knitting and hold the tail out of your way for the first few stitches. Knit one row using the new yarn.

4 At the end of the row, join the next strand of yarn in the same way and knit one row.

5 Add on the next three coloured strands in the same way.

6 Take the final, longer strand of yarn and join it in as usual. Knit one row.

7 Cast off but do not sew in the loose ends.

Materials

● A selection of different coloured fine yarns, such as fingering-weight cotton, glittery crochet thread or embroidery thread. You will need six 1m (3ft) lengths and one 1.5m (5ft) length for the bracelet, and seven 1m (3ft) lengths and one 2m (7ft) length for the choker

- - - - - - - - - - - - - - - -

● 4mm knitting needles

- - - - - - - - - - - - - - - -

● Scissors

- - - - - - - - - - - - - - - -

● Masking tape

Braiding the ties

1 Lay the knitted strip on a flat surface and straighten out all the loose ends.

2 Use a piece of masking tape to hold the middle of the strip securely on the surface.

3 Braid all the loose strands at one end of the bracelet for about 5cm (2in) to make a tie. If you need a reminder of how to do braiding, look back at page 17.

Tie a knot at the end of the braid and trim it neatly.

4 Knot the end of the braid securely and trim to leave the ends about 2cm (1in) long.

5 Repeat Steps 3–4 at the other end of the bracelet.

Now that you have the hang of them, these friendship bands can be knitted in any width. Just use more or fewer stripes.

Eight-stripe choker

1 Design a stripe pattern to coordinate with the bracelet. Remember that the final strand needs to be longer than the rest.

2 Start with a 1m (3ft) length of yarn. Make the cast-on slip knot about 25cm (10in) from the beginning of the yarn and cast on 46 stitches.

3 Tie the second coloured strand in a knot around the first strand of yarn, leaving a 25cm (10in) tail before the knot.

4 Follow Steps 3–4 of Knitting the Bracelet until you have added in the five remaining 1m (3ft) lengths of yarn.

5 Take the final, 2m (7ft) length of coloured yarn and join it in as usual. Knit one row.

6 Cast off but do not sew in the loose ends.

7 Braid the ties in the same way as you did for the bracelet, but this time make them about 8cm (3in) long.

Mini-knitting brooches

You can make this cluster of unusual brooches by knitting on tiny, doll-sized needles. When you wear them, all of your friends will be amazed that you can knit so small. The two mini knitting needles are made from cocktail sticks and beads. All you need to do is cast on as usual and knit.

> Knitting on tiny needles is exactly the same as using ordinary needles, just much smaller, so you can still refer to pages 24–31 if you need a reminder of how to do something.

Mini-needles brooch

This brooch consists of a miniature pair of knitting needles and a tiny ball of yarn, so it looks like someone is halfway through a piece of knitting. It's simple to make, takes hardly any time and even less yarn, and you don't need to cast off!

Making mini needles

1 Choose two cocktail sticks to make the needles. These can be traditional wooden ones or you could find colourful plastic versions.

2 Find a pair of beads to form the knobs at the end of each needle. The hole in the bead should be the right size to fit onto the stick.

▲ Dip the stick in some glue, then push it into the hole of the bead.

3 Dip the tip of one stick into a small amount of craft glue and insert it into the hole in one of the beads. Hold the stick and bead together for a few minutes to let the glue set a little.

4 Wipe away any excess glue and allow to dry thoroughly. Repeat for the other needle.

Materials

- At least 2m (7ft) of fine yarn, such as fingering-weight cotton, crochet thread or embroidery thread

- 2 cocktail sticks

- 2 beads, about 5–10mm (¼in) diameter

- Craft glue

- Scissors

- 5 x 25mm (¼ x 1in) strip of paper and some sticky tape

- Brooch clip or safety pin

- Tapestry needle

Mini knitting

1 Take a fine yarn and cast on ten stitches with the mini needles.

△ Use your mini needles to knit ten rows.

2 Using the knit stitch on every row, knit ten rows. You will need to have at least 60cm (24in) of yarn left.

3 Do not cast off. Leave the knitting on the needle.

4 Put the empty needle safely to one side for the moment.

Making the mini ball of yarn

△ Wrap the yarn around two of your fingers to make a mini ball of yarn.

1 Cut the yarn so that you have about 60cm (24in) left. Starting 5cm (2in) from the knitting, wind the yarn loosely around and around two of your fingers, making a mini ball of yarn.

△ Wrap the end of the yarn tightly around the middle of the ball.

2 Wrap the last 5cm (2in) of the yarn firmly around and around the middle of the ball, to hold it tight.

△ Wrap a strip of paper around the yarn to look like a ball band.

3 Wrap the strip of paper around the tiny ball and use a little bit of adhesive tape to keep it in place. This looks like a ball band and will hold the yarn in place.

Fixing the brooch to the clip

△ Stitch a brooch clip or safety pin to the back of the knitting.

1 The brooch clip or safety pin must be fastened near the top of the knitting, on the back. You can use a tapestry needle and some spare yarn to stitch over the clip or pin and into the back of the knitting.

△ If your clip has a flat surface, you can glue it in place instead.

2 If the clip has a flat surface, you may be able to use craft glue to hold it in place. Whichever method you use, make sure that the brooch looks neat from the front.

3 Get the empty needle that you put to one side and push it through the piece of knitting.

Well done! Now you can wear your brooch and impress everyone with your great new knitting skills.

Project 4

Mini knitted hat and scarf brooches

Now that you have the hang of miniature knitting, you can make another pair of mini knitting needles and knit this fun pair of brooches.

Materials

● About 7m (25ft) of fine yarn, such as fingering-weight cotton, crochet thread or embroidery thread

----

● Pair of mini knitting needles, like you made on page 38

● Scissors

● Tapestry needle

● 2 brooch clips or safety pins

Making the scarf

1 On the mini knitting needles, cast on four stitches as usual. Knit 30 rows.

2 Cast off and sew in the ends on the wrong side. The wrong side is the side where you're going to attach the brooch clip or safety pin when you've finished knitting.

3 Now make the fringing. This is like the fringing on the Funny-face Bag on page 34, but you will need to use a tapestry needle instead of a crochet hook because the stitches are so small. First, cut eight 10cm (4in) lengths of fine yarn.

▲ Use a tapestry needle to thread fringing through the end of the scarf.

4 Fold a length of yarn in half and thread the folded end through a tapestry needle. Stitch it through the end of the scarf to the wrong side and remove the needle, leaving the yarn in the knitting.

5 Carefully thread the ends of the fringing through the loop and pull to secure.

▲ Trim the fringing neatly.

6 Repeat Steps 4–5 to make four fringes at each end of the scarf, then trim the ends.

7 Carefully attach the scarf to a brooch clip or safety pin, like you did on page 39.

Making the hat

1 On the mini knitting needles, cast on eight stitches as usual. Leave an 20cm (8in) tail of yarn at the beginning of the row.

2 Knit 20 rows. Cast off, but don't sew in the loose ends.

▲ Sew a few small stitches to hold the turn-up in place.

3 Thread the tail at the cast-on end onto a tapestry needle and fold the first three rows of knitting up to the right side. The right side is the side that you want to face outward when you're wearing the brooch. Make a few tiny stitches into the turn-up to hold it in place.

4 Sew in the loose ends on the wrong side.

▲ Add a tassel at each corner and in the centre of the top of the hat.

5 To make a tassel, cut three 20cm (8in) lengths of the fine yarn. Use a tapestry needle to make three fringes, like you did in Steps 4–6 of Making the Scarf, one at each corner and one in the centre of the cast-off row.

Small is fun!

Braid the tassel and tie a knot at the end to keep the braid secure.

6 Braid the fringe tightly for about 1cm (¼ –½in). If you need a reminder of how to do braiding, look back at page 17. The braid will gather in the top of the hat. Tie the ends securely with a double knot, then trim the ends evenly.

7 Carefully attach the hat to a brooch clip or safety pin, like you did on page 39.

Mini-knitting brooches

You could also make mini-knitting hair clips that will look great in your hair.

Fantastic flowers

Make bouquets of these amazing knitted brooches and you can use them to decorate sweaters, bags or bedrooms. This is a chance to experiment with sparkly, fancy yarns and fluffy mohair, and to add on sequins and beads. The more exotic, the more colourful, the better!

To make these flowers, you will be using the skills you learned on pages 24–31, so you can always look again at the instructions and pictures there if you need a little extra help.

Giant mohair flower

This is a really fun way to make your first flower. It is knitted in fluffy mohair yarn and decorated with sequins and a giant bead.

Materials

- About 16m (50ft) of mohair yarn
- About 1.5m (5ft) of mohair yarn in a contrasting colour
- 8mm knitting needles
- Scissors
- Tapestry needle
- Mohair brush or an old, clean toothbrush
- Giant bead
- Assorted sequins
- Sewing thread and needle
- Brooch clip or safety pin

Knitting the flower

1 Cast on 40 stitches. Knit each stitch on every row for 12 rows.

2 Cast off, leaving a tail of yarn about 20cm (8in) long.

Something sparkly!

Running stitch

1 Thread a tapestry needle with the tail of yarn.

2 You now need to gather the centre of the flower using a running stitch. This is an easy way of gathering up knitting. Push the needle down through the last stitch of the cast-off edge.

3 Now skip a stitch and bring the needle back up through the next stitch of the cast-off edge.

▲ Sew a running stitch along the cast-off edge of your knitting.

4 Stitch all along the edge in the same way, pushing the needle into every other stitch.

▲ Pull one end of the yarn to gather the knitting into a circle shape.

5 When you get to the end of the row, gently pull the yarn through until the cast-off edge is completely gathered up.

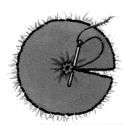

▲ Sew a few stitches through the centre to hold the circle in place.

6 Stitch back through the gathered knitting to secure the thread.

Sewing the seam

1 The gathered edge will be the centre of the flower. Bring the two open sides of the knitting to meet each other and make a circular flower shape.

▲ Use oversewing stitch to sew the open edge of the circle closed.

2 Using the thread already on the needle, stitch the open sides of the flower together. You can use a small oversewing stitch to do this, as you did on page 34 with the Funny-face Bag. Sew the seam on the wrong side of the flower.

3 Sew in the loose ends on the wrong side.

Brushing the mohair

▲ Gently brush the mohair to make it more fluffy.

1 Mohair always looks much fluffier if it is brushed after being knitted. Using a mohair brush or an old, clean toothbrush, gently brush the front of the knitting from the centre of the flower out to the edge.

Embroidering the loopy centre

1 The loopy stitch centre of this flower looks really good if it is stitched with mohair yarn in a colour that contrasts with the main flower. Thread a tapestry needle with about 1.5m (4½ft) of yarn and knot the ends together so you have a double strand.

2 Pull the needle and thread through a stitch near the centre of the flower from the back to the front.

▲ Wrap the yarn around three of your fingers to make a loop.

3 Place three fingers in the centre of the flower. Pass the yarn over your fingers and stitch back down through the centre of the flower, forming a loop of yarn over your fingers. Slip your fingers out of the loop.

▲ Make a small stitch to secure the loop to the centre of the flower.

4 Bring the needle back through to the front and make a small stitch through to the back. This will secure the loop.

5 Repeat Steps 2–4 to make five more loops.

6 Sew a double stitch with the yarn at the back of the flower to secure it, then cut the yarn.

Decorating the flower

▲ Sew a giant bead in the centre of the flower.

1 Put a giant bead in the centre of the flower and sew it in place. You will probably need to use ordinary sewing thread and a sewing needle at this stage, because the yarn and tapestry needle will both be too thick.

2 A few carefully placed sequins can transform plain knitting. You can choose a sewing thread to match either the sequins or the knitting, or go for a gold or silver thread for something very decorative. Thread the sewing needle and tie a knot in the other end of the thread.

3 Decide where you want to put the sequin. Stitch up from the back of the knitting, passing the needle through a strand of yarn so the knot holds.

▲ Thread the needle through a sequin.

4 Pass the needle through the hole in the sequin.

5 Slide the sequin down the thread until it touches the knitting.

▲ Let the thread go over the top of the sequin and stitch through to the back.

6 Pass the thread over the sequin and stitch back into the knitting just behind the sequin.

7 Bring the thread back up through the hole in the sequin and back down into the knitting on the other side of the sequin.

▲ Bring the needle to the front where you want to sew another sequin.

8 Get ready to sew the next sequin in place and bring the needle through to the front of the knitting in the position you have chosen.

9 Repeat Steps 4–8 until you have sewn on all the sequins. Make a few tight stitches into the back of your knitting to secure the thread, then trim it.

10 Now that you have finished the flower, attach it to a brooch clip or safety pin like you did with the Mini-knitting Brooches on page 39.

Rosette flower

This flower uses two different coloured glittery crochet threads. Choose colours that you think look exciting together and decorate the flower with sequins to make it even more sparkly.

Outside rosette

1 Take the first colour of glittery crochet thread and cast on 14 stitches. Knit 120 rows.

2 Cast off, leaving a 30cm (1ft) tail of yarn. Thread the yarn onto a tapestry needle.

▲ Sew a running stitch along one edge and pull it tight to form a circle.

3 Gather up the long edge of the knitting using a running stitch, like you did on page 43 with the Giant Mohair Flower.

▲ Stitch the open edge of the circle shape closed.

4 Stitch the cast-on and cast-off ends of the strip together using a small oversewing stitch on the back of the flower.

5 Sew in the ends of the yarn on the back of the flower.

Materials

- About 28m (90ft) of glittery crochet thread in the first colour
- About 10m (35ft) of glittery crochet thread in the second colour
- 4mm knitting needles
- Scissors
- Tapestry needle
- Button or bead
- Assorted sequins
- Sewing thread and needle
- Brooch clip or safety pin

Centre rosette

1 Now take the second colour of glittery crochet thread and cast on eight stitches. Knit 70 rows.

2 Cast off, leaving a 30cm (1ft) tail of yarn. Thread the yarn onto a tapestry needle.

3 Gather and stitch just as you did in Steps 3–5 of knitting the Outside Rosette.

Assembling the flower

1 Place the smaller rosette in the centre of the larger rosette.

▲ Stitch the small rosette onto the centre of the large rosette.

2 Take some more of the crochet thread you used for the small rosette and thread about 30cm (1ft) onto a tapestry needle. Stitch the two rosettes together close to the centre, ending with the needle at the back of the flower. Make a few small stitches to secure.

3 Thread the needle through the very centre of the flower from back to front and sew on a button or bead. If the needle doesn't fit through the hole in the button or bead, you may need to use a sewing needle and thread for this stage.

4 Decorate the rosette with sequins, like you did with the Giant Mohair Flower on page 44. Then you can fix it to a brooch clip or safety pin. Look back at page 39 of the Mini-knitting Brooches project to see how to do this.

Just look at the fantastic flower you have made. Did you ever think you could make such cool things with knitting?

Loopy flower

This flower is made using a long piece of spool knitting. A fine mohair will work well, but you can experiment with other kinds of yarn, such as double-knitting yarn.

1 Make a 120cm (4ft) length of spool knitting. Look back at page 15 if you need a reminder of how to do this. Cast off the end, leaving a tail of yarn about 30cm (1ft) long.

▲ Wrap your length of spool knitting around the strip of cardboard.

2 Position one end of the spool knitting at the bottom edge of the strip of cardboard. Wrap the knitting around and along the cardboard strip, making ten loops and finishing with the other end of the knitting at the bottom of the cardboard. Thread the tail of yarn onto a tapestry needle.

3 Lay the cardboard on a flat surface to hold the knitting in position. Push the loops close together.

▲ Stitch through each of the loops on the cardboard.

4 Stitch through the first loop of knitting and pass the needle through the knitting of all the remaining loops, working along the bottom edge of the cardboard and finishing with the cast-on end of the knitting.

5 Remove the cardboard and pull the yarn tight, gathering all the loops together.

6 Stitch back into the first loop so that you have made a loopy flower shape.

▲ Sew a few stitches through the centre to secure the flower shape.

7 Secure the flower shape by stitching a few times into the centre. Sew in the ends of the yarn and trim them.

8 Stitch a bead or button into the centre of the flower. You will probably need to use ordinary sewing thread and a sewing needle at this stage, since the yarn and tapestry needle will both be too thick.

9 Attach the flower to a brooch clip or safety pin like you did with the Mini-knitting Brooches on page 39.

Materials

- About 25m (85ft) of double-knitting or mohair yarn
- Spool knitter
- Scissors
- Strip of cardboard, 6 x 25cm (2½ x 10in)
- Tapestry needle
- Large bead or button
- Sewing thread and needle or craft glue

Something sparkly!

Now that you know how easy it is to make flowers, you can combine different techniques and yarns to create your own inventions. What about a loopy mohair flower with a small, sparkly rosette centre?

Supersize scarf

This scarf may be big, but you will be amazed at how quickly you can knit it. In contrast to the tiny brooch on page 40, but using the same basic knit stitch, this scarf is knitted on big needles with big yarn. You can personalize it with your own name written in huge letters from a length of spool or finger knitting, or you could sew shapes such as hearts and stars onto the scarf instead. It would even look pretty without any extra decoration.

The knitting skills you learned on pages 24–31 are used in this project, so refer to the instructions and pictures there if you have forgotten anything.

Huge and huggable!

Beginning the scarf

1 Cast on 18 stitches with the main, super chunky yarn. Knit each stitch in every row. Remember to keep the working end of the yarn taut while you are knitting. The scarf is a great project for practising how to do this because it's so big. Look back at pages 26–29 if you need a reminder.

2 Continue knitting rows of knit stitch until your ball of yarn is about to run out.

Starting a new ball of yarn

▲ Knot the new yarn around the old yarn at the beginning of a row.

1 You will need to start a new ball of yarn when the one you are using is about to run out or if you want to change to a different colour (for example, when knitting stripes). Always try to start a new ball of yarn at the beginning of a row, because it is more difficult to get a neat join in the middle of a row. Cut the yarn that you are finishing, leaving a tail of about 10cm (4in). Tie the new yarn around the tail.

2 Slide the knot up close to the knitting, then tighten the knot. Begin knitting with the new ball of yarn that you have just joined in.

More knitting

1 Continue knitting rows of knit stitch until your scarf is about 1.5m (5ft) long, or as long as you want it to be, if you have enough yarn. If you want, you can just keep knitting and knitting!

2 Cast off, but be especially careful not to cast off too tightly when knitting with this super chunky yarn. Make sure the cast-off edge is as loose and stretchy as the giant knitting.

3 Sew all the loose strands of yarn coming from the scarf into the wrong side. Remember to sew in the loose strands from where you started a new ball.

Materials

● 200m (220yds) of super chunky yarn for the scarf

● Yarn in a contrasting colour for the letters. You will need about 50m (55yds) of super chunky yarn for a short name like the one shown in this project, or up to 100m (110yds) of a fine yarn such as fingering-weight cotton for a longer name

● Either 30m (35yds) of super chunky yarn or 80m (90yds) of fine yarn for the fringing, depending on which you prefer

● 15mm knitting needles

● Scissors

● Tapestry needle

● Spool knitter

● Crochet hook

● Cardboard, about 12cm (5in) square

● Pins

'Garter stitch' is a term you may come across as you do more knitting. It simply means that every row is stitched with the knit stitch. So, this scarf has been made in garter stitch.

Picking up dropped garter stitches

If you accidentally drop a stitch while you are knitting, you can pick it up and no one will ever know. Try to pick up a dropped stitch as soon as possible or it will keep running farther down (if it does run, see pages 121–122).

▲ Put the right needle through the dropped stitch from back to front.

1 Put the tip of the right needle through the dropped stitch, going from back to front.

▲ Put the right needle under the strand from back to front.

2 Insert the tip of the right needle under the strand, going from back to front.

▲ Use your left needle to lift the dropped stitch over the strand.

3 Use the point of your left needle to lift the dropped stitch over the strand and drop it off the right needle, like casting off. The new stitch is now on the right needle.

▲ Slip the new stitch onto your left needle and knit it in the usual way.

4 Insert the point of the left needle into the new stitch from front to back and slip the stitch onto the left needle, ready to be knitted as usual.

Writing your name

1 You can use either spool knitting or finger knitting to write your name. Look back at pages 14–15 to remind yourself how to do this. If the yarn you are using is fine, you can make strips of spool knitting. If it is chunky, you can use finger knitting instead.

2 You will need to use strips of knitting to make up each element of the letters. For example, the letter T needs two strips – one for the vertical line and one for the horizontal line that goes across the top. Practise writing on the scarf with strands of yarn to see how long each strip needs to be.

3 Make strips of finger or spool knitting the right length for each

letter of your name. Remember to cast off at the end of each piece so that it will not unravel.

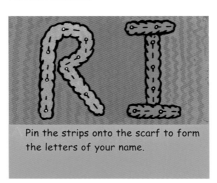
Pin the strips onto the scarf to form the letters of your name.

4 Lay the scarf on a flat surface and pin the strips into place to make your name. Adjust the positioning until you are happy with how it looks.

• •

Slip stitching the writing into place

1 Slip stitch is often used for sewing one piece of knitting on top of another because the stitching will not be seen from the outside. Thread a tapestry needle with a spare piece of the yarn used for the writing. Make a knot at the end of the yarn.

2 Starting at the beginning of the first letter, gently lift the edge of the strip of spool knitting or finger knitting.

Lift up the edge of the strip and sew the back of it to the scarf.

3 Make a stitch into the back of the strip and take the needle down and through the loop of the nearest stitch on the front of the scarf. Do not stitch right through to the wrong side of the scarf, and make sure that you do not pull the stitches too tight.

4 Bring the needle back up through the knitting, catch it into another stitch on the back of the strip, and down to the nearest stitch on the scarf.

5 Follow Steps 3–4 to continue attaching the underside of the strip to the scarf.

Stitch all along each length of spool or finger knitting.

6 Repeat Steps 2–5 to attach each strip for every letter. At the end of each strip, secure the stitching by sewing twice into the last stitch. Sew in the strands of yarn so that they are hidden.

Huge and huggable!

Making the fringing

1 Your scarf is nearly finished. All you need to do is add some decorative fringing at both ends. You could use the same colour as the scarf or the writing, or mix them together. You can use a piece of cardboard to help you measure the lengths of fringing really evenly. About 12cm (5in) square is a good size, but you can experiment with longer or shorter fringing if you wish. Wrap the yarn around and around the cardboard.

Cut through the yarn along one edge of the cardboard to make the fringing.

2 Cut in a straight line across the lengths of yarn at one edge of the cardboard, so that you make a pile of strands all the same length.

3 Add fringing to both ends of your scarf, as you did for the Funny-face Bag on page 34.

This is the biggest thing that you have knitted so far. Your supersize scarf is now ready to wear.

Making shapes

You've knitted some fabulous things already but all your knitting has been square or rectangular. It's now time to learn how to make different shapes by increasing and decreasing stitches. Increasing means adding stitches to make your fabric wider; decreasing means taking stitches away to make your fabric narrower. You can try out these shaping techniques to make a wobbly fried egg, a curved belt and a triangular headscarf.

Increasing

Increasing is a technique that shapes the knitting by adding stitches. You add stitches to make your knitting wider. There are several different ways to increase. The method you use will depend on how many stitches you want to add and where you want to add them. The cable method is the simplest way of adding one or more extra stitches at the beginning of a row. The bar increase method is good for adding a single stitch anywhere on a row.

Remember that the 'working end' of the yarn is the end that comes from the ball.

Cable increase

The cable increase can be used only at the beginning of a row. You can use it to add one or more stitches.

1 Insert the tip of the right-hand needle between the first two stitches on the left-hand needle.

3 Draw a loop through with the right-hand needle.

2 Using your index finger, wrap the working end of the yarn from behind the right-hand needle, from left to right, passing the yarn between both needles.

Increasing the yolk

You are now going to practise using the bar increase method of adding stitches.

1 **Row 2:** At the beginning of Row 2, increase one stitch using the bar increase method on the first stitch. Knit the next four stitches, then increase one stitch using the bar increase method on the last stitch. You now have eight stitches on your needle.

2 **Rows 3–4:** Knit all eight stitches on both these rows.

3 **Row 5:** At the beginning of Row 5, increase one stitch using the bar increase method on the first stitch. Knit the next six stitches. Increase one stitch using the bar increase method on the last stitch. You now have ten stitches.

4 **Rows 6–9:** Knit the next four rows. You have now knitted nine rows.

5 **Row 10:** At the beginning of Row 10, increase one stitch using the bar increase method on the first stitch. Knit the next eight stitches. Increase one stitch using the bar increase method on the last stitch. You now have 12 stitches.

6 **Rows 11–18:** Knit the next eight rows. Well done. You have already knitted 18 rows and it's time to start decreasing.

Decreasing the yolk

You are going to practise the knit 2 together method to decrease the stitches on the yolk.

1 **Row 19:** At the beginning of Row 19, knit the first two stitches together. Knit the next eight stitches.

Knit the last two stitches together. You now have ten stitches.

2 **Rows 20–23:** Knit all ten stitches on the next four rows.

3 **Row 24:** At the beginning of Row 24, knit the first two stitches together. Knit the next six stitches. Knit the last two stitches together. You now have eight stitches on your needle.

4 **Rows 25–26:** Knit all of the stitches on the next two rows.

5 **Row 27:** At the beginning of Row 27, knit the first two stitches together. Knit the next four stitches. Knit the last two stitches together. You now have six stitches.

6 **Row 28:** Knit all stitches on the next row. Cast off.

Congratulations! The yolk is ready. What a great shape. Now let's knit the egg white.

Starting the egg white

1 Cast on nine stitches using white yarn and the cable cast-on method.

2 **Row 1:** Knit all of the stitches on the first row.

Increasing the egg white

You are about to practise the cable increase method of adding stitches.

1 **Row 2:** At the beginning of Row 2, increase two stitches using the cable increase method. Knit to the end of the row. You now have 11 stitches.

2 **Row 3:** Knit all of the stitches on the third row.

3 **Row 4:** At the beginning of Row 4, increase two stitches using the cable increase method. Knit to the end of the row. You now have 13 stitches.

4 **Row 5:** Knit all of the stitches on the fifth row.

5 **Rows 6–10:** Increase one stitch at the beginning of each row using

the cable increase method. Knit to the end of each row. You will now have 18 stitches.

6 **Row 11:** At the beginning of Row 11, increase two stitches using the cable increase method. Knit to the end of the row.

7 **Row 12:** At the beginning of Row 12, increase one stitch using the cable increase method. Knit to the end of the row.

8 **Row 13:** At the beginning of Row 13, increase two stitches using the cable increase method. Knit to the end of the row. You can probably now see the wobbly shape being made by

sometimes increasing by one stitch and other times increasing by two stitches.

9 **Row 14:** At the beginning of Row 14, increase one stitch using the cable increase method. Knit to the end of the row. You now have 24 stitches.

10 **Rows 15–25:** Knit all of the stitches on the next 11 rows.

11 **Rows 26–28:** Increase one stitch at the beginning of each row using the cable increase method. Knit to the end of each row. You now have 27 stitches.

12 **Rows 29–40:** Knit all of the stitches on the next 12 rows.

Decreasing the egg white

We are now ready to start decreasing the egg white. This time we will use the cast-off decrease to reduce stitches.

1 **Row 41:** At the beginning of Row 41, decrease one stitch using the cast-off decrease method. Knit to the end of the row.

2 **Rows 42–45:** Knit all of the stitches on the next four rows.

3 **Rows 46–54:** Decrease one stitch at the beginning of each row using the cast-off decrease method.

Knit to the end of each row. You now have 17 stitches.

4 **Rows 55–56:** Decrease two stitches at the beginning of each row using the cast-off decrease method. Knit to the end of each row. You now have 13 stitches.

5 **Rows 57–58:** Decrease three stitches at the beginning of each row using the cast-off decrease method. Knit to the end of each row.

6 Cast off all seven remaining stitches of the egg white.

Fantastic work! You have knitted a wobbly egg white. Now let's sew the yolk onto the white.

Assembling the fried egg

1 Lay the wobbly egg white on a flat surface and decide where to position the yolk.

2 Put a small ball of stuffing or cotton wool behind the yolk. This will make it bulge realistically.

3 Pin the yolk in place, making sure that the stuffing is hidden from view.

▲ Sew the yolk to the centre of the egg white with an oversewing stitch.

4 Thread a tapestry needle with 30cm (12in) of leftover yellow yarn, and use a small oversewing stitch, like you did with the Funny-face Bag on page 34, to stitch the yolk neatly into place.

5 Neaten all the loose ends by sewing them in with the tapestry needle.

Now that your fried egg is ready, only you can decide what to do with it. You could stitch it onto a knitted scarf or bag, using white yarn and oversewing stitch.

Or is the floppy Frisbee going to become the next playground craze?

Let's get cooking!

Alternatively, you could serve up a knitted fried egg as a practical joke on April Fool's Day!

Desert island belt and headscarf

This project is knitted in soft, natural coloured cotton yarn or string, with wooden beads and braided ties. The use of odd-sized needles and knotting creates a trendy, handcrafted macramé effect. You could try using parrot-coloured cottons and sparkly beads for a psychedelic paradise island version.

This time you will be using the bar increase and the knit 2 together decrease techniques to shape your fabric. Look back at the pictures and instructions on pages 54–56 if you are not sure how to do the techniques. We will also continue using the knitting skills learned on pages 24–31 and 57.

Wavy belt

To make the curvy shape of the belt, you simply repeat a basic pattern of decreasing and increasing stitches.

Starting the belt

1 Cast on ten stitches using the cable cast-on technique.

2 Knit the first six rows using knit stitch on every row.

Castaway fashion!

Materials

- 40m (45yds) of double-knitting cotton yarn
- 5mm knitting needles
- Scissors
- Tapestry needle
- Crochet hook
- 72 wooden beads with holes big enough to thread the cotton yarn through

Curvy shaping

1 You are going to begin shaping the belt using the knit 2 together decrease. At the beginning of the next row, knit the first two stitches together, making the two stitches into one stitch. Now knit the next two stitches together in the same way. Continue to knit two stitches together all along the row so that you finish with five stitches on the right-hand needle.

2 Knit the next eight rows without decreasing any stitches.

3 You are now going to increase the number of stitches again. At the beginning of the next row, increase one stitch using the bar increase method on the first stitch.

Now use the same bar increase method on each stitch of the row. You now have ten stitches on the right needle.

Increase the number of stitches to make the belt shape curve outward.

4 Knit the next six rows without increasing any stitches.

You will see that the pattern of decreasing and increasing is what makes the wavy shape of the belt. It couldn't be easier.

Making the belt the right length

Do enough curvy shapes so that the belt is long enough to fit around your waist.

1 You need to continue knitting to this pattern, following Steps 1–4 of Curvy Shaping, until the belt is just the right length. To make a belt that will fit a 60–70cm (24–28in) waist, repeat the decrease and increase shaping five more times. If you want to make the belt to fit a smaller person, measuring 50–60cm (20–24in), knit just four more shapings. Or, to fit a larger

person, measuring 70–80cm (28–32in), knit six more shapings.

2 Cast off all ten stitches, sew in the loose ends and trim.

You have now made the main part of the belt. All you need to do next is make the ties, embellished with hippie beads.

Castaway fashion!

Braided ties

1 Cut nine 80cm (32in) lengths of cotton yarn. Fold each length in half and use them to make fringes evenly spaced along the edge of the cast-on row, just like you did for the Funny-face Bag on page 34.

△ Thread two beads onto each fringe.

2 Thread two beads onto each of the nine fringes of yarn.

△ Push a bead up the right-hand fringe and start braiding.

3 Make a braid with the first three fringes (six strands of yarn). If you need a reminder, look at braiding on page 17. You need to push the beads up the fringe one by one so that they become worked into the braid. Start by pushing one bead to the top of the right-hand fringe, then move the rest of the right fringe over to the middle.

△ Push a bead up the left-hand fringe and continue braiding.

4 Now push one bead to the top of the left-hand fringe, then move the rest of the left fringe over to the middle.

△ Push a bead up the new right-hand fringe and continue to braid.

5 Push one bead up the new right-hand fringe as far as the crossover point (this is the point where another fringe of yarn crosses over it), then move this fringe over to the middle.

△ Push another bead up the left-hand fringe and keep braiding.

6 Push a bead up the left-hand fringe to the crossover point, then move the left fringe over to the middle.

△ Push another bead up the right-hand fringe and keep braiding.

7 Push a bead up the right-hand fringe as far as the crossover point, then move the right fringe over to the middle.

△ Push the final bead up the left-hand fringe and finish braiding.

8 Push the final bead up the left-hand fringe to the crossover point, then move the left fringe over to the middle.

△ Separate the strands into two halves and tie a knot below the beads.

9 When all six beads are braided in, divide the six strands of yarn into two groups of three, and tie in a knot to secure the braid.

10 Now braid the next three fringes in the same way and secure with a knot. Then braid the final three fringes in the same way and secure these with a knot.

Make two braids with the rest of the yarn.

11 Divide the strands of yarn below the three knots into two halves and braid each half for 15cm (6in), tying the end of each braid with a knot to secure.

Push a bead onto the end of each strand of yarn, tie a knot and trim.

12 Now thread a bead onto each individual strand of yarn and tie a double knot below it to keep the bead from falling off. Trim the yarn ends.

You have finished one end of the belt and doesn't it look funky? Now make the decorative braids at the other end in exactly the same way.

Castaway headscarf

This headscarf uses a combination of thick and thin knitting needles to make loose knitted stripes, using the knit stitch that you have been practising.

Starting the headscarf

1 Cast on 50 stitches using the cable cast-on technique and 5mm knitting needles.

2 Rows 1–2: Work the first two rows in knit stitch.

Materials

- 40m (45yds) of double-knitting cotton yarn
- 5mm knitting needles
- One 15mm knitting needle
- Scissors
- Tapestry needle
- Crochet hook
- 12 wooden beads with holes big enough to thread the cotton yarn through

Shaping the headscarf

1 You are going to use the knit 2 together decrease to shape the scarf.
Row 3: At the beginning of Row 3, knit the first two stitches together. Knit to the last two stitches, then knit the last two stitches together. You have decreased two stitches and now have 48 stitches on the needle.

2 **Row 4:** Decrease at both ends of the row as in Row 3, leaving 46 stitches.

Knit the next row using the large needle to make big, loose stitches.

3 **Row 5:** This row is referred to as the loose row. Put down the empty 5mm knitting needle and use the big 15mm needle to knit this row. Decrease at both ends of the row as before, leaving 44 stitches.

4 **Row 6:** Using the 5mm needle, knit this row, decreasing at both ends of the row as before, leaving 42 stitches when you have finished.

5 **Rows 7–9:** Put down the 15mm needle and use both 5mm needles to knit three rows, decreasing at both ends of each row. You will now have 36 stitches and nine rows.

6 **Row 10:** Now it's time for another loose row. Knit this row like Row 5, using the 15mm needle and decreasing at both ends. You will now have 34 stitches.

7 **Rows 11–14:** Repeat Rows 6–9, always decreasing at both ends of each row. You will now have 26 stitches.

8 **Row 15:** This is another loose row. Knit this row like Row 5, using the 15mm needle and decreasing at both ends. You will be left with 24 stitches.

9 **Rows 16–19:** Repeat Rows 6–9 again, always decreasing at both ends of each row. You will now have 16 stitches left.

10 **Row 20:** You've guessed it, another loose row. Knit this row like Row 5, using the 15mm needle and decreasing at both ends, leaving 14 stitches.

11 **Row 21:** Using the 5mm needle, knit this row, decreasing at both ends of the row as before, leaving 12 stitches.

Just like with the belt, you can now see the basic shape of the headscarf, and all that remains to be added are the ties and the beads.

12 Row 22: Now you are going to bring in another loose row, but without decreasing. So, using the 15mm needle, knit all the stitches.

13 Rows 23–28: Repeat Rows 21 and 22 three more times. You should now have six stitches on your needle and 28 rows.

14 Row 29: With the 5mm needle, decrease at the beginning and end of the row, leaving four stitches.

15 Cast off all the stitches and sew in the loose ends.

Braided ties

1 Cut six 40cm (16in) lengths of cotton yarn.

2 Take three lengths and use a crochet hook to thread them through one corner of the headscarf at the cast-on edge.

3 Braid the strands together for about 12cm (5in). Look back to page 17 if you need to jog your memory about braiding. Tie a knot at the end of the braid to secure it.

Make a beaded braid at each corner of the cast-on edge of the scarf.

4 Thread a bead onto the end of each strand and tie a double knot below it to keep the bead from falling off. Trim the ends of the yarn.

5 Now do the same at the other corner of the scarf and you have finished.

If you are going on a beach vacation this year, don't forget to take these accessories. Everyone will want to know where you bought them!

Making stitch patterns

This chapter teaches you a new stitch – the purl stitch. It is a bit different from the knit stitch and, when you mix the two together, you can make all kinds of new textures. Learn to purl and you'll be able to make rib, stocking stitch and moss stitch. It's also time to learn other new skills, like knitting holes, making ladders and knitting in the round.

Purl stitch

Now that you have mastered the knit stitch, you are ready to learn the purl stitch. Knit and purl stitches can be combined in a number of different ways to make a wonderful variety of patterns. Once you have mastered the purl stitch, there will be no limits to what you can create.

Using a smooth yarn, practise working rows of purl stitch until you really have the hang of it. Take as much practice as you need so that you can make the projects on the following pages look really special.

1 Cast on 10 to 20 stitches using the cable cast-on method shown on page 57.

2 Hold the needles and yarn in the same way as for making a knit stitch, but with the working end of the yarn at the front of the needles this time.

3 Insert the right-hand needle from right to left into the front of the first stitch on the left needle so that the two needles cross each other with the right needle in front.

4 Using your index finger, wrap the working end of the yarn from right to left over the tip of the right needle. The yarn starts and finishes in front of the needles. If you're holding the yarn in your right hand, it will look like this.

5 If you're holding the yarn in your left hand, make a stitch in exactly the same way, but use your left index finger to wrap the yarn around the right needle.

6 Lower the tip of the right needle and draw it away from you through the centre of the stitch on the left needle, together with the loop of yarn. This loop will be your new stitch.

7 Pull the right needle up so that you can drop the original stitch off the left needle, keeping the new stitch on the right needle.

8 Congratulations: you have made your first purl stitch. To purl a row, repeat Steps 3–7 until all the stitches have been moved from the left needle to the right needle.

9 Now, to make another purl row, swap the needles so that the one with all the stitches is in your left hand and the empty needle is in your right hand, and start again from Step 3. Make sure that the yarn is in front of the needles before you start and remember to keep the yarn taut while you purl.

10 Continue purling each row until you have had enough practice, then cast off in the usual way.

● ●

Stitch patterns

While you are practising, you will probably notice that the front of the purl stitch looks like the back of the knit stitch, and vice versa. See how the front of a knit stitch forms a V shape and the back forms a loop shape. Now look at how it's the front of a purl stitch that forms a loop shape and the back that forms a V shape. Different stitch patterns are made by using different combinations of these V shapes and loops. The patterns pictured here are called stocking stitch (above right) and reverse stocking stitch (below left), which you'll learn on page 73.

▶ **Front of knit stitch looks like back of purl stitch**

◀ **Front of purl stitch looks like back of knit stitch**

Silly sausages

This silly string of sausages gets longer and longer as you practise different stitch patterns. Stuff them, surprise somebody, or squirt ketchup on them! So far, all the projects have been made using the knit stitch. Now it's time to learn more about the purl stitch and discover how to get textured or stretchy effects in your knitting. Making this long strip of knitting will give you a chance to practise new stitch patterns that combine the purl and the knit stitches.

This project combines knit stitch and purl stitch, so you will be using the knitting skills you learned on pages 24–31 and 70–71. You will also be using the decreasing and cable cast-on techniques on pages 56–57. If you need a reminder of how to do something, simply glance back to the pictures and instructions on those pages.

Sausage 1 – single rib

Materials

- 150m (165yds) of double-knitting yarn
- 4mm knitting needles
- Scissors
- Tapestry needle
- Stuffing

This sausage uses a pattern of stitches called single rib. This is made by knitting one stitch, then purling one stitch. It creates a stretchy fabric that pulls in very narrow. It is often used for the trims on the bottom edges, cuffs and collars of garments. The single rib pattern looks exactly the same on both sides of the knitting. Some other stitch patterns have a right side and a wrong side, so it is important to know which is the right side of your knitting when you are combining different stitch patterns.

1 Cast on 28 stitches using the cable cast-on technique. When knitting single rib for the first time, it is easiest to cast on an even number of stitches, so the pattern is the same for every row.

▲ Bring the yarn to the front, ready to do a purl stitch.

2 Row 1: Knit the first stitch. Bring the yarn to the front of the knitting between the needles. Purl the next stitch.

▲ Take the yarn to the back, ready to do a knit stitch.

3 Take the yarn between the needles to the back and knit the next stitch.

4 Bring the yarn to the front again and purl the next stitch.

5 Repeat Steps 3–4, taking the yarn back to knit one stitch, then forward to purl one stitch, until you have finished the row. The last stitch will be a purl.

6 Row 2: Knit one stitch then purl one stitch to the end of the row, exactly the same as Row 1, ending with a purl stitch.

7 Repeat this row until your single ribbing is about 15cm (6in) long.

8 Don't cast off. You can continue to knit the next stitch pattern with the same yarn.

Sausage 2 – stocking stitch

This sausage uses stocking stitch. This is the pattern of working one row of knit stitch and one row of purl stitch alternately. Stocking stitch is one of the most commonly used stitches because it makes a smooth fabric, which is known as stockinette. You will see that whenever you are working a knit stitch row, the right side of the stockinette is facing you. The purl side is known as reverse stockinette. It looks a bit like garter stitch but the ridges are smaller.

▲ When you do a knit row, the right side of your knitting is facing you.

1 Row 1: When you are knitting Row 1 of stocking stitch, the right side of your knitting will be facing you. Knit all stitches for the first row.

2 Row 2: Purl all stitches for the second row. You will see that the wrong side of your knitting is facing you now.

▲ When you do a purl row, the wrong side of your knitting is facing you.

3 Repeat Steps 1–2 until your stockinette is about 15cm (6in) long. Make sure that the last row is a purl row with the wrong side facing you.

▲ The single rib of the first sausage will pull in the stockinette.

4 You will notice that the single rib that you knitted first pulls in the stockinette. Don't worry. Although you have the same number of stitches in a row, the different stitch patterns will knit up to different widths. This can be useful, especially when shaping knitted clothes.

5 Check that you still have 28 stitches on your needle and you will be ready to knit the next sausage.

Sausage 3 – double rib

Knit two stitches, purl two stitches – that's how easy it is to make double rib. Double rib is stretchy, like single rib, but gives wider vertical lines of stitches. It looks the same on the right and wrong sides. It also pulls in the stockinette.

1 **Row 1:** Knit the first and second stitches. Bring the yarn to the front, just like you did in Step 2 of Sausage 1, and purl the next two stitches.

2 Repeat these four stitches along the row, remembering to take the yarn to the back before knitting two stitches and bring the yarn to the front before purling two stitches. The last two stitches will be purl.

3 **Row 2:** Repeat Row 1. You will see that you are knitting into the purl stitches of the previous row and purling into the knit stitches. This is always how you make a rib.

▲ Knit two stitches, then purl two stitches all along each row.

4 Repeat Steps 1–3 until you have about 15cm (6in) of double rib.

Sausage 4 – garter stitch

If you purl all your rows, the knitting looks exactly the same as the garter stitch that you have been using for projects until now. It looks the same on the right and wrong sides.

1 **Row 1:** Purl all the stitches on the first row.

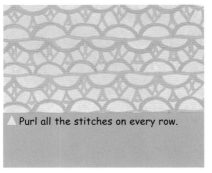

▲ Purl all the stitches on every row.

2 Continue to purl all rows until the purl knitting measures about 15cm (6in). You should still have 28 stitches on your needles.

Sizzling patterns!

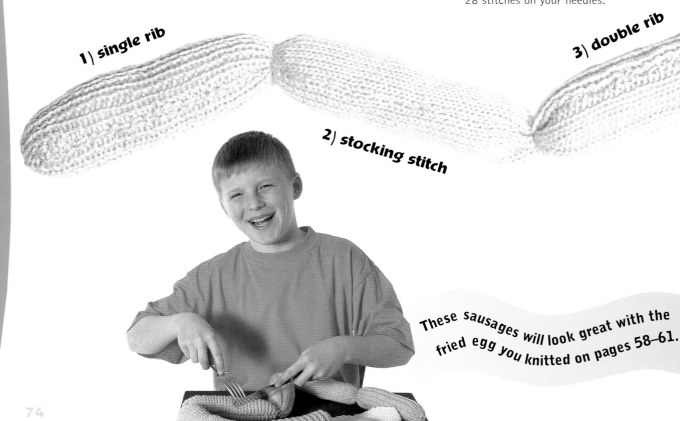

1) single rib

2) stocking stitch

3) double rib

These sausages will look great with the fried egg you knitted on pages 58–61.

Sausage 5 – moss stitch

This sausage uses moss stitch. Like single rib, but with an odd number of stitches, moss stitch makes a firm fabric that has the same bumpy texture on both sides. It doesn't curl up at the edges, so it is often used for edges and bands.

1 Moss stitch is easiest when knitted with an odd number of stitches in a row, so you need to decrease one stitch at the end of the first row, leaving 27 stitches on your needle.

Row 1: Knit into the first stitch. Bring the yarn to the front as usual and purl into the next stitch. Take the yarn to the back again. Continue to knit one stitch, purl one stitch until you reach the last two stitches. Knit two stitches together to decrease one stitch, like you did on page 56.

2 Row 2: Knit one, purl one to the end of the row. The last stitch will be a knit.

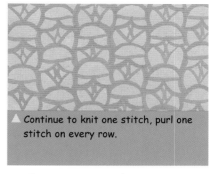

▲ Continue to knit one stitch, purl one stitch on every row.

3 Repeat Row 2 until your moss stitch sausage is about 15cm (6in) long.

5) moss stitch

4) garter stitch

6) ridged

Sausage 6 – ridged

The ridges on this sausage are simply stripes of stocking and reverse stocking stitch. This fabric spreads wide and shrinks up short. It is reversible, because the pattern looks the same on both sides of the fabric.

1 Row 1: Knit one row.
Row 2: Purl one row.
Row 3: Purl one row.
Row 4: Knit one row.

▲ Make a ridged sausage by using rows of knit and purl stitches.

2 Repeat these four rows until the ridged knitting is about 15cm (6in) long.

3 Cast off all the stitches. You have now completed all six sausages.

Backstitch seam

Backstitch makes a strong seam and is good for lighter weight yarns. It can be a bit bulky if used with thick yarns.

1 Thread a tapestry needle with a spare length of yarn. Fold the knitting in half lengthways, with right sides facing, making sure that the stitches are matching row for row.

2 Starting with the first row of knitting at the right-hand end, make two strong oversewing stitches to join the first stitches together and fix the end of the yarn.

▲ Bring the needle up between Row 1 and Row 2.

3 Keeping exactly one stitch from the edge, bring the needle up through both pieces of knitting between the stitches of the first and second rows.

▲ Push the needle back down between Row 1 and the cast-on edge.

4 Push the needle down between the first row and the cast-on edge.

5 Bring the needle up between the second and third rows.

▲ Push the needle back down between Row 1 and Row 2.

6 Push the needle down between the stitches of the first and second rows, where the previous stitch started.

7 Bring the needle up two more rows, between the third and fourth rows.

▲ Push the needle back down between Row 2 and Row 3.

8 Push the needle back down where the previous stitch started, between the second and third rows.

9 Continue in the same way to make a continuous line of stitches on the side of the knitting facing you.

▲ Secure the end of the seam with a couple of oversewing stitches.

10 When you reach the end of the side seam, use oversewing stitches to fasten the yarn end.

Stuffing the sausages

▲ Turn your knitting right side out, so that the seam stitching is hidden.

1 Now that you have a long tube, the next stage is to turn the knitting right side out. Use your fingers or the blunt end of a knitting needle to push the knitting through.

▲ Sew a running stitch around one of the open ends.

2 Thread a tapestry needle with more spare yarn and make a running stitch around one of the open ends to gather it up, just like you did when making the Giant Mohair Flower on page 43. Pull the yarn tight, knot securely and trim the ends.

3 Push some stuffing right down into the tube until you have filled the first sausage. Roll the sausage between your hands to even out the stuffing.

▲ Sew a running stitch at the end of the stuffed sausage.

4 Sew a running stitch along the last row of the stuffed sausage. Pull tight, knot the yarn tightly, sew in the ends and trim.

5 Repeat Steps 3–4 with each sausage until you complete the whole string.

You have learned lots of new stitches and made a silly string of sausages. Now it's time to swing them around and show all your friends what fun knitting can be.

Cosmic clutch bag

With this sparkly purse, sprinkled with tiny holes and spangled with giant sequins, you'll be the star of the galaxy. This bag looks great knitted in double-knitting yarn mixed with glittery crochet thread, but you can follow the pattern with almost any yarn – just use the needles recommended on your yarn band. You will be using stocking stitch and learning to make yarnover holes.

To make more interesting items, you need to start using all your new knitting skills together, but don't worry if that sounds daunting. Just remember to look at the pictures and instructions on pages 24–31, 54–57 and 70–71 if you need extra help with any of the techniques.

Yarnovers

A yarnover is a way of increasing an extra stitch and at the same time creating a decorative hole. Yarnovers are used when knitting lace and also for making eyelets and buttonholes. A yarnover is often used in combination with a decrease, to make a hole without adding any stitches to the row. You may want to practise making a few yarnover holes with some oddments of yarn before you start the bag.

Bring the yarn to the front of your knitting.

Wrap the yarn over the top of the right needle and continue knitting.

Purl all the stitches on the next row, including the new yarnover stitch.

1 Knit as far as the place where you want to make the yarnover. Bring the yarn to the front of your knitting, between the needles, as if you were about to purl a stitch.

2 Wrap the yarn over the top of the right needle and knit the next stitch. The wrapped yarn becomes a new stitch.

3 On the next row, make sure that you purl the new stitch.

Galaxy of glitter!

Materials

- 100m (110yds) of double-knitting yarn in the main colour
- 25m (30yds) of double-knitting yarn in a contrasting colour
- 100m (110yds) of glittery crochet thread in the main colour
- 25m (30yds) of glittery crochet thread in a contrasting colour
- 5mm knitting needles
- Scissors
- Tapestry needle
- Pins
- Button
- 4 or 5mm crochet hook
- Sequins
- Sewing thread and needle

Stocking stitch

If you are confident at doing yarnovers, let's get started on the project. The bag is knitted in stocking stitch, which you practised when you made the Silly Sausages on page 73.

1 Hold the ends of the contrast colour double-knitting yarn and contrast colour glittery crochet thread together. Make a single slipknot using both pieces of yarn. Cast on 45 stitches, using both yarns together as if they were one yarn.

△ Make sure you work every stitch with both yarns together.

2 Work one row in knit stitch. Be careful that you always work with both yarns together throughout the project.

3 Work the second row in purl stitch, again making sure that you use both yarns.

△ Count the lines of Vs to check how many rows you have knitted.

4 You will remember from the Silly Sausages project that one row knit and one row purl makes stocking stitch. Continue knitting in stocking stitch until you have 20 rows. It is easy to count rows of stocking stitch because each row looks like a line of Vs.

5 Now change to the main colour, again mixing the double-knitting yarn and glittery crochet thread together. Look at page 48 of the Supersize Scarf to remind yourself how to tie in a new yarn. Work 60 rows in stocking stitch, ending on a purl row. Do not cast off.

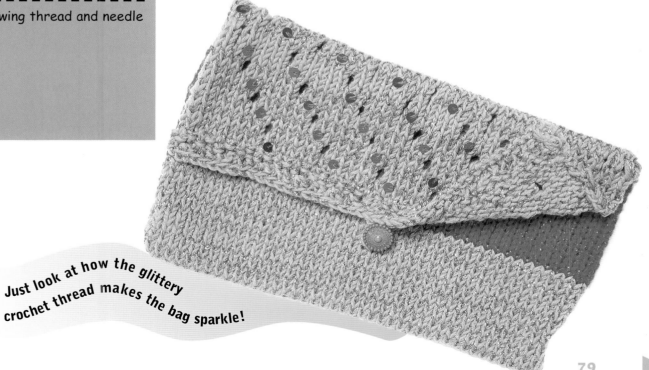

Just look at how the glittery crochet thread makes the bag sparkle!

Picking up dropped stocking stitches

Picking up dropped stocking stitches involves a different technique from the one you learned for picking up garter stitches on page 49. (If the stitch runs and makes a ladder, see pages 94–95.)

On a knit row

▲ Keep the knit side facing you when you pick up the stitch.

1 Hold the knitting with the knit side facing you.

▲ Insert the right needle through the dropped stitch and under the strand from front to back.

2 Insert the tip of the right-hand needle through the dropped stitch, from front to back, and then under the strand above it in the same way, from front to back.

Use the left needle to pass the picked-up stitch over the strand.

3 Use the point of the left needle to lift the picked-up stitch and pass it over the strand. Now slip the stitch off the needle, just like casting off, leaving the repaired stitch on the right needle.

Slip the repaired stitch onto the left needle.

4 Put the tip of the left needle through the repaired stitch from front to back and slip the stitch onto the left needle, ready to be worked in the usual way.

On a purl row

Keep the purl side facing you when you pick up the stitch.

1 Hold the piece of knitting with the purl side facing you.

Insert the right needle through the dropped stitch and under the strand from back to front.

2 Insert the tip of the right needle through the dropped stitch, from back to front, and then insert the tip of the needle under the strand above it the same way, from back to front.

Use the left needle to pass the picked-up stitch over the strand.

3 Use the point of the left needle to lift the picked-up stitch and pass it over the strand. Now slip the stitch off the needle, just like casting off, leaving the repaired stitch on the right needle.

Slip the repaired stitch onto the left needle.

4 Put the tip of the left needle through the repaired stitch from front to back and slip the stitch onto the left needle, ready to be worked in the usual way.

Lace pattern

To make the lace-hole patterned flap of the bag, you will be using the knit 2 together decrease, then making a yarnover.

1 This is the first lace pattern row. **Row 81:** *Knit four stitches, then knit the next two stitches together. Now bring the yarn forward to make a yarnover.* Repeat the pattern between the asterisks six more times, then knit the last three stitches.

2 **Row 82:** Purl all stitches, making sure that you purl into all the yarnover loops and still have 45 stitches at the end of the row.

3 **Row 83:** Knit all stitches.
Row 84: Purl all stitches.

4 This is the second lace pattern row. **Row 85:** Knit two stitches, then knit the next two stitches together. Bring the yarn forward to make a yarnover. *Knit four stitches, then knit the next two stitches together. Now bring the yarn forward to make a yarnover.* Repeat the pattern between the asterisks five more times, then knit the last five stitches.

5 **Row 86:** Purl all stitches.
Row 87: Knit all stitches.
Row 88: Purl all stitches.

6 This is the third lace pattern row. **Row 89:** *Knit four stitches, then knit the next two stitches together. Now bring the yarn forward to make a yarnover.* Repeat the pattern between the asterisks six more times, then knit the last three stitches.

7 **Row 90:** Purl all stitches.
Row 91: Knit all stitches.
Row 92: Purl all stitches.

8 This is the fourth lace pattern row. **Row 93:** Knit the first six stitches, then knit the next two stitches together.

Bring the yarn forward to make a yarnover. *Knit four stitches, then knit the next two stitches together. Now bring the yarn forward to make a yarnover.* Repeat the pattern between the asterisks five more times, then knit the last stitch.

9 **Row 94:** Purl all stitches.
Row 95: Knit all stitches.
Row 96: Purl all stitches.

10 This is the fifth lace pattern row. **Row 97:** Knit the first eight stitches, then knit the next two stitches together. Bring the yarn forward to make a yarnover. *Knit four stitches, then knit the next two stitches together. Now bring the yarn forward to make a yarnover.* Repeat the pattern between the asterisks four more times, then knit the last five stitches.

11 **Row 98:** Purl all stitches.
Row 99: Knit all stitches.

Asterisks

As you work through this project, you will often come across a pair of asterisks (small stars) surrounding a set of instructions within the pattern. This saves on having to spell out the whole sequence again when it needs repeating. Instead, the pattern will tell you to repeat the stitches between the asterisks. For example: *Knit two stitches, purl two stitches.* Repeat two more times. This means knit two, purl two, knit two, purl two, knit two, purl two. Just imagine how much space it would take if you had to write out the sequence 20 times!

Moss stitch trim

1 Check that you still have an odd number of stitches on your needle – you should have 45 in total.
Rows 100–102: *Knit one stitch. Purl one stitch.* Repeat along the row, ending with a knit stitch.

2 Cast off all the stitches, sew in the loose ends and trim.

Phew! Now that the main part and the flap are done, let's start adding the trimmings and sewing it up.

Sewing the seams and button

1 Fold the bag right sides together so that the cast-on edge nearly reaches the first lace-hole row. Use a few pins to hold it in place.

Backstitch the side seams.

2 With a tapestry needle and the main colour of double-knitting yarn, backstitch both side seams securely, like you did on page 76 of the Silly Sausages project.

Sew a button to the front of the bag in the centre.

3 Turn the bag right side out. Use the same yarn to stitch a button in the centre of the front of the bag, so that it sits just below the flap.

Crocheting the loop

Put a slipknot onto the crochet hook.

1 You now need to use a crochet hook to make a chain loop for fastening the button. Crochet is just like finger knitting, but finer. Make a slipknot with the main double-knitting yarn and put it onto the crochet hook.

Push the hook through a stitch at the edge of the flap in the centre.

2 Push the tip of the hook through a stitch at the centre of the last row of knitting on the flap.

Wrap the yarn around the hook.

3 Wrap the yarn around the tip of the crochet hook.

Pull the yarn through the stitch and the slipknot.

4 Use the hook to pull the yarn through the stitch and the slipknot, making a loop on the crochet hook. This is the first stitch.

5 Wrap the yarn around the tip of the hook and pull it through the first stitch. This is the second stitch.

Make a chain of stitches to fit around the button.

6 Repeat Step 5 to continue making a chain of stitches until it is long enough to go around the button.

7 Cut the thread, leaving a 15cm (6in) tail of yarn.

8 Use the hook to pull the end of the yarn right through the last stitch and pull to tighten.

82

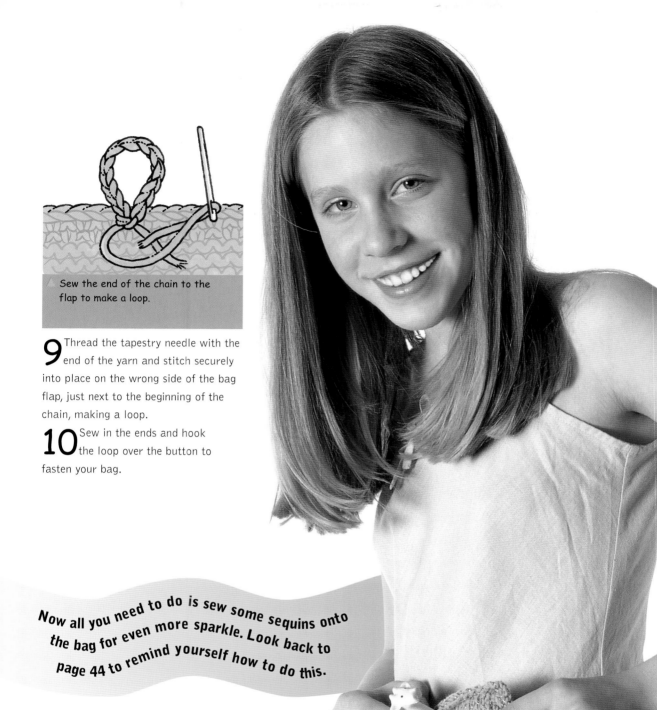

Sew the end of the chain to the flap to make a loop.

9 Thread the tapestry needle with the end of the yarn and stitch securely into place on the wrong side of the bag flap, just next to the beginning of the chain, making a loop.

10 Sew in the ends and hook the loop over the button to fasten your bag.

Now all you need to do is sew some sequins onto the bag for even more sparkle. Look back to page 44 to remind yourself how to do this.

Floppy dollies

Make a cute and cuddly doll with floppy arms and legs, or swap the braided hair for pointy ears and, hey presto, you have a bunny! These dolls use simple shaping techniques in stocking stitch and, when they are finished, you can knit miniature clothes with oddments of yarn.

To make these dolls, you need to use nearly all the knitting skills you have learned so far. From now on, we will no longer tell you which increase or decrease method to use, just like in real knitting patterns. So, if you forget anything, look back at the pictures and instructions on pages 24–31, 54–57 and 70–71 for a bit of extra guidance.

Floppy doll

Front

Start your floppy doll by knitting the front piece, working from the legs up to the head.

Knitting the first leg

1 Cast on eight stitches in the shoe yarn on 4mm needles.

2 **Row 1:** Knit one row.
Row 2: Purl one row.

3 **Row 3:** Knit one row, increasing one stitch at the beginning and one stitch at the end of the row.

4 **Rows 4–9:** Repeat Rows 2 and 3 three more times, until you have 16 stitches and nine rows on your needle.
Row 10: Purl one row.

5 Change to the body yarn and work in stocking stitch to Row 50. Look at page 48 of the Supersize Scarf to remind yourself of how to tie in a new yarn.

6 Trim the yarn, leaving a 15cm (6in) tail. You now need to put the stitches onto a stitch holder or large safety pin while you knit the other leg.

Knitting the second leg

1 Cast on eight stitches in the shoe yarn and work exactly as you did for the first leg as far as Row 50. Don't forget to change colour on Row 11.

2 **Row 51:** Knit across the 16 stitches and then cast on two stitches. Put the needle to one side for a moment.

3 You now need to put the stitches from the stitch holder back onto the empty 4mm knitting needle. When all the stitches are on the needle, put the needle in your left hand and put down the stitch holder.

Body

△ Knit across the stitches you picked up from the stitch holder to join the legs together.

1 **Row 1:** Pick up the other needle (the one holding the second leg) in your right hand and knit across the stitches that you have just picked up from the stitch holder. Pull the yarn tightly as you knit into the first stitch so that you get a neat join. Both legs are now hanging from the same needle and you have 34 stitches on the needle.

2 **Row 2:** Purl all stitches.
Rows 3–18: Starting with a knit row, continue working all stitches in stocking stitch for 16 more rows.

Using a stitch holder

When knitting some patterns, you will need to leave stitches on a stitch holder to be worked into at a later stage. A stitch holder looks like a large safety pin with a blunt point.

1 To put stitches onto a stitch holder, hold the needle with the stitches in your left hand. Insert the tip of the stitch holder into the first stitch.

▲ Slip the stitches from the left needle onto the stitch holder.

2 Slip the stitch from the left needle onto the holder. Work along the row of stitches, one by one, in the same way. When the required number of stitches are on the holder, close it and put it safely aside.

3 To pick up stitches from a stitch holder when you need to use them again, hold the stitch holder in your left hand. Hold the empty needle in your right hand and insert the needle into the first stitch on the stitch holder.

4 Slip the stitch from the holder onto the right needle. Work along the row of stitches, one by one, in the same way. When the required number of stitches are on the needle, put the needle in your left hand and put down the stitch holder.

Materials

- 180m (200yds) of double-knitting yarn for the body
- 10m (11yds) of double-knitting yarn for the shoes
- 25m (30yds) of double-knitting yarn for the hair
- 60m (70yds) of double-knitting yarn in various colours for the dress
- 4mm knitting needles
- 5mm knitting needles
- Stitch holder or large safety pin
- Scissors
- Tapestry needle
- 2 toy eyes or buttons plus 2 buttons for the dress
- Oddments of yarn for embroidery
- Pins
- Stuffing
- Crochet hook

3 **Row 19:** You are now going to shape the shoulders. Knit one row, decreasing one stitch at the beginning and one stitch at the end of the row.
Row 20: Purl one row.

4 **Rows 21–40:** Repeat Rows 19 and 20 for 20 more rows. When you have finished, you will have 12 stitches on your needle.

Neck and head shaping

1 **Rows 1–4:** Work four rows in stocking stitch.

2 **Rows 5–10:** For the next six rows of stockinette, increase one stitch at the beginning and one stitch at the end of each row. You will have 24 stitches on your needle.

3 **Rows 11–22:** Work 12 rows of stocking stitch with no shaping.

▲ Decrease at each end of the rows to shape the top of the head.

4 **Rows 23–30:** For the next eight rows of stocking, decrease one stitch at the beginning and one stitch at the end of each row. You will have eight stitches left on your needle.

5 **Row 31:** Knit one row and cast off all the stitches.

Back

Follow all the steps in the Front section to knit the back exactly the same as the front.

Arms

You need to make two arms in exactly the same way, working in stocking stitch and starting with the hands.

Shaping the hands

1 Cast on ten stitches in the body yarn on 4mm knitting needles.

2 **Row 1:** Knit one row.
Row 2: Purl one row.

3 **Row 3:** Knit one row, increasing one stitch at the beginning and one stitch at the end of the row.
Row 4: Purl one row.

4 **Rows 5–12:** Repeat Rows 3 and 4 four more times, giving you 20 stitches and 12 rows.

5 **Row 13:** Knit one row.
Row 14: Purl one row, decreasing one stitch at the beginning and one stitch at the end of the row.

6 **Row 15:** Knit one row, decreasing one stitch at the beginning and one stitch at the end of the row, leaving 16 stitches.

7 **Row 16:** Purl one row.
Row 17: Knit one row.
Row 18: Purl one row.

Shaping the arm

1 **Rows 19–22:** Increase one stitch at the beginning and end of each row for the next four rows of stocking stitch. You will have 24 stitches and 22 rows.

⚠ Use stocking stitch to lengthen the shaped arm.

2 **Rows 23–44:** Work another 22 rows of stocking stitch to Row 44. Do not increase or decrease on these rows.

3 Cast off all the stitches. Remember to knit a second arm in exactly the same way.

Assembling the doll

Adding the face

Sew on some toy eyes or buttons and a smiley mouth, like you did for the Funny-face Bag on pages 32–33, using a tapestry needle and oddments of yarn.

Sewing and stuffing

⚠ Sew the front and back together, leaving the top of the head open.

1 Put the back and front together, right sides facing, and use pins to hold the pieces in position. Using a tapestry needle and the main body yarn, backstitch the pieces together around the edge, like you did on page 76 of the Silly Sausages project. Leave the cast-off edges at the top of the head open. Remove the pins.

▲ Stuff the body, then sew the top of the head closed.

2 Turn the doll right side out, then fill the body with stuffing. Use a knitting needle to push it right down the legs. Use a small version of the oversewing stitch that you learned on page 34 to close the opening at the top of the head.

3 Fold one arm in half lengthways, right sides facing, and backstitch the side seam with the main yarn, leaving the top open. Turn right side out. Repeat with the other arm.

▲ Stuff the arms, then sew the tops closed.

4 Fill the arms with stuffing and use a small oversewing stitch to close them up.

▲ Sew the arms to the body.

5 Sew the arms securely in place on the body using oversewing stitches.

Making the hair

1 Cut lots of strands of the hair yarn, each about 25cm (10in) long.

▲ Use a crochet hook to pull a bunch of hair through the top of the head.

2 Take a bunch of five or six strands and use a crochet hook to pull one end of the strands through the knitting at the top of the head.

▲ Tie a knot next to the head to hold the hair in place.

3 Pull the yarn through until both ends are even, then tie in a knot next to the head to hold it in place.

4 Repeat Steps 2–3 five mores times, so that you have six bunches of hair across the top of the head.

▲ Make two braids and tie the ends with colourful yarn.

5 Braid three bunches of hair on one side of the head, then braid the remaining three bunches of hair on the other side of the head. If you need any help, look back at the braiding technique on page 17. Tie the ends of the two braids with a length of yarn in a contrasting colour.

Wow! Isn't it great to be able to knit your own toys? Now that your floppy doll is complete, you can decide on her name while you knit her a little dress.

Knitting a dress

The doll's dress is knitted in stripes of different coloured yarns. You can use any stripe pattern that you like.

Knitting the stripes

1 On 5mm knitting needles, cast on 68 stitches in the dress yarn and work four rows in knit stitch.

2 Using a 4mm needle, purl one row.

△ Knit stripes of colour on the dress.

3 Now bring in the other 4mm needle and begin knitting stocking stitch, changing colour whenever you like. Look at page 48 of the Supersize Scarf to remind yourself of how to tie in a new yarn. Knit 22 rows of stocking stitch.

4 Now work four rows in single rib (knit one stitch, purl one stitch). Cast off.

Knitting the straps

1 Cast on five stitches on 4mm needles and knit 70 rows in garter stitch (knit all stitches).

2 Cast off and make another strap in the same way.

Assembling the dress

1 Backstitch the back seam, as you did for the doll.

2 Put the dress onto the doll and pin the straps into place. They should cross over each other and tuck inside the dress at the back, and sit on the outside of the dress at the front.

△ Sew the crossed-over straps inside the back of the dress.

3 Slip the dress off the doll and use a tapestry needle and spare yarn to stitch the straps into place at the back of the dress.

△ Sew a button onto each strap at the front of the dress.

4 Place a button on each strap where it overlaps the dress at the front and sew the button into place through the strap and the dress.

Floppy bunny

Materials

● 200m (220yds) of double-knitting yarn for the body and outside ears

● 20m (25yds) of double-knitting yarn for the paws and inside ears

● 30m (35yds) of double-knitting yarn for the tail

● 10m (15yds) of orange double-knitting yarn for the carrot tie

● 4mm knitting needles

● Stitch holder or large safety pin

● Scissors

● 2 toy eyes or buttons

● Tapestry needle

● Oddments of yarn for embroidery, including green

● Pins

● Stuffing

● Two 5cm (2in) diameter cardboard discs with 2.5cm (1in) diameter holes for pompom making

● 10cm (4in) of narrow elastic

Now put the dress back on the doll and admire your handiwork. If you are feeling up to the challenge, why not make the bunny as well?

Happy playmates!

Body and arms

Knit the front of the body in exactly the same way as you knit the floppy doll, but knit the legs in the main colour only because bunnies don't wear shoes! Knit the back in the same way as the doll, starting with the paw colour for the first ten rows of the legs. Knit the arms just like you did for the doll.

Floppy ears

You need to make two ears alike. Remember to knit the outside and inside ears in different colours.

Outside ear

1 Cast on 18 stitches using the body colour yarn.

2 **Row 1:** Knit all stitches.
Row 2: Purl all stitches.

3 **Row 3:** Knit one row, increasing one stitch at the beginning and one stitch at the end of the row.
Row 4: Purl all stitches.

4 **Rows 5–10:** Repeat Rows 3 and 4 three more times, giving you 26 stitches on your needle.

5 **Rows 11–22:** Work 12 rows in stocking stitch, giving you 22 rows.

6 **Row 23:** Knit one row, decreasing one stitch at the beginning and one stitch at the end of the row.
Row 24: Purl all stitches.

7 **Rows 25–44:** Repeat Rows 23 and 24 ten more times. When you have finished, you will have four stitches left on the needle.

8 Cast off. Remember to make a second outside ear in exactly the same way.

Inside ear

1 Cast on eight stitches using the inside ears yarn.

2 Work 30 rows in stocking stitch (one row knit, one row purl).

3 **Row 31:** Knit one row, decreasing one stitch at the beginning and one stitch at the end of the row.
Row 32: Purl all stitches.

4 Repeat Rows 31 and 32 until you have only one stitch left.

▲ Make two outside ears and two inside ears.

5 Cast off the last stitch. Remember to make a second inside ear in exactly the same way so that you have two outside and two inside pieces.

Assembling the bunny

Follow the instructions for Assembling the Doll. Don't add the hair, of course; the bunny needs ears and a tail instead.

Adding the face

1 Use a tapestry needle and a scrap of yarn to sew some toy eyes or buttons on the front of the head. (The front is the piece of knitting without the paws.)

△ Sew the mouth just below the eyes in the centre of the face.

2 Sew a big X for the mouth and do a little stitch over the centre to hold it in place.

Adding the ears

1 Pin the inside ear piece flat onto the main ear with wrong sides facing and the cast-on edges touching.

△ Stitch the inside ear piece onto the centre of the outside ear piece.

2 Using the main body yarn and the tapestry needle, stitch the two pieces together around the edges of the inside ear piece. The edges of the outside ear piece will roll around to make a good shape.

△ Sew the tips of the ears into a pointy shape.

3 Sew the edges at the tips of the outside ear piece together to make them pointed.

△ Sew the bottom edges together to make the ears curvy.

4 Fold the bottom edges of the ear inward until they touch each other and stitch into place.

△ Stitch the ears to the top of the head.

5 Pin the ears into place on the head and stitch securely, like you sewed the arms.

Adding the tail

Make a pompom following the instructions on page 16, but don't trim the tied ends of yarn. Thread the ends onto a tapestry needle and use them to stitch the tail securely into place on the bunny's bottom.

Carrot tie

A carrot tie is all that is needed to dress up the rabbit. The tie is knitted in garter stitch, where all rows are knit stitch.

Knitting the tie

1 Cast on three stitches in orange yarn. Knit one row.

2 Increase one stitch at the beginning of the next eight rows until you have 11 stitches.

3 Knit eight rows without increasing any more stitches.

4 Decrease one stitch at both ends of the next row so that you have nine stitches.

5 Knit three rows without decreasing any more stitches.

6 Decrease one stitch at both ends of the next row.

7 Knit nine rows of seven stitches. Cast off.

Making the knot for the tie

1 Cast on six stitches. Work 16 rows in knit stitch. Cast off.

Assembling the tie

△ Stitch the knot to the tie with small, neat stitches.

1 Fold the knot in half and stitch it to the top of the tie.

△ Attach some elastic to the back of the knot big enough to fit over the bunny's head.

2 Thread a piece of elastic through the back of the knot on the tie. Tie the ends of the elastic together, then check that it will fit over the bunny's head. Undo the knot and try again if it doesn't. When the knot's in the right place, trim the ends of the elastic.

△ Make a green leafy tassel at the tip of the tie.

3 Cut a few short pieces of green yarn and pull them through the tip of the tie with a crochet hook to make a leafy tassel.

The doll and bunny make a great pair. Perhaps you could knit them to give as a present to a younger sister, brother, cousin or friend.

Check this out!

Project 12

Plaid poncho

This poncho will dazzle everybody with its colour and pattern. It is knitted in horizontally striped stocking stitch with no shaping. To create the plaid effect, just drop some stitches on the last row of knitting and watch them run! Then weave contrast colours through the ladders to create the vertical lines. Finish off with fringing. The poncho measures 45cm (18in) from neck to wrist, before the fringing is added.

Remind yourself of the skills needed to knit this poncho by looking at pages 24–31, 57 and 70–71.

Measuring tension

When knitting items of clothing, it's important for your piece of knitting to end up the right size so that it fits you. To check that the size will be okay, you need to knit a test piece about 12 x 12cm (5 x 5in), following the instructions of the main knitting pattern and using the recommended needle size. You then count the number of stitches and rows in the test piece. This is called measuring the tension. All knitting patterns tell you how many stitches and rows you should have across a certain measurement.

1 To knit a test piece for the poncho, cast on 30 stitches and follow the pattern instructions for Steps 1–3 of Knitting the Poncho Front, until it measures about 12cm (5in) long.

▲ Count the number of stitches between the pins.

2 Lay a ruler across the width of the test piece. Push a pin through the knitting at the beginning of the ruler and then push another pin into the knitting 10cm (4in) across. Remove the ruler and count how many stitches (V shapes) there are between the two pins. Write the number down and remove the pins.

3 Measure 10cm (4in) down the length of the test piece, using pins to mark the knitting like you did in Step 2. Remove the ruler and count how many rows there are between the pins. An easy way to count rows is to

▲ Count the number of rows between the pins.

count from the point of one V shape to the point of the next. Write the number down and remove the pins.

4 The tension for this poncho is 22 stitches to 10cm (4in) and 28 rows to 10cm (4in). If your test piece has more stitches and rows than this, you will need to use larger needles than the pattern says. If your test piece has fewer stitches and rows than this, you will need to use smaller needles than the pattern says.

5 Knit another test piece with the new size needles and measure it like before. Keep trying until you get the right size.

92

Fringing

Add some fringing around the bottom of the poncho, just like you did for the Funny-face Bag on page 34. Cut lots of 30cm (1ft) lengths of yarn and use six strands at a time, using a crochet hook to add a tassel of fringe every 5cm (2in) all around the edge.

Any double-knitting yarns will work for this poncho. Try using a fluffy yarn for the stripes and fringing to create a more unusual effect.

Peruvian pompom hat

For this colourful hat, you're going to use different coloured yarns in stripes to create your own design. Try varying the widths of the stripes from one row to about six. The fun part of making this hat is that you get to work on circular and double-pointed needles. This is called 'knitting in the round'. You can also practise moss stitch, blanket stitch and, best of all, you can top it off with big rainbow-coloured pompoms!

Remind yourself of the skills needed to knit this hat by looking at pages 16–17, 24–31, 54–57 and 70–71.

Making the hat

▲ Cast 96 stitches onto the circular needle.

1 Cast 96 stitches onto the circular needle. Slip a stitch marker onto the needle after you have cast on the last stitch.

2 **Round 1:** Purl into the first cast-on stitch so that your knitting forms a round circle. Continue to purl into each stitch until you reach the stitch marker – you have now knitted a round. Slip the stitch marker onto the other needle. Make a note on some

paper each time you finish a round (as you reach the marker) so that you know how many rounds you have knitted.

3 **Rounds 2–4:** Purl three more rounds. You have now knitted four rounds. Look at the knitting – you'll see that you are knitting reverse stocking stitch.

4 Change colour for the next stripe. Keep changing colour every so often – wherever you like – to create more stripes.

5 **Rounds 5–24:** Knit for 20 more rounds. You will now use knit stitch for the rest of the knitting but, amazingly, you'll see that knitting in rounds gives stocking stitch.

6 **Round 25:** This is where you begin to decrease. Knit 22 stitches, then knit two stitches together and put a second colour stitch marker onto the needle. Repeat this step until you reach your original stitch marker.

7 You have now decreased a total of four stitches, so you should have 92 stitches on your needle.

8 **Round 26:** Knit the next round without decreasing, slipping the stitch markers onto the next needle as you come to them.

9 **Round 27:** Now knit 21 stitches. You will see that there are two stitches left before you reach the marker – knit these two together and then slip the marker onto the next needle. Repeat this whole step three more times. You now have 88 stitches on your needle.

10 **Round 28:** Knit this round without decreasing, slipping the stitch markers to the next needle as you come to them.

Materials

- 240m (265yds) of double-knitting yarn in assorted colours
- 4mm circular needle of 60cm (2ft) in length
- Four 4mm double-pointed needles
- Two 4mm single-pointed needles
- Pencil and paper
- Cardboard discs for pompom making
- Tapestry needle

Making a stitch marker

A stitch marker will help you see when you have finished a round of knitting or need to decrease. You can buy stitch markers or make your own. To make one, cut 5cm (2in) of yarn in a colour that you will not be using in your knitting. Tie it into a loop around your needle, making sure that it doesn't grip too tightly. When you reach the stitch marker in your knitting, do not knit into it but just slip it onto the next needle and continue to knit the next stitch.

Tension

20 stitches to 10cm (4in)
28 rows to 10cm (4in)
(see Measuring Tension, page 92)

11 **Round 29:** For this round, you need to knit 20 stitches. You will see that there are two stitches left before you reach the marker. Knit these two stitches together. Slip the stitch marker onto the next needle. Repeat this whole step three more times. You now have 84 stitches on your needle.

12 Keep knitting your work in rounds, decreasing on every other round, each time knitting one stitch less in between decreasing. Just remember to knit together the last two stitches before each marker and you won't need to count stitches.

13 You've probably noticed that as you've decreased the stitches, the knitting won't reach properly around the circular needle any more. So now you need to transfer the knitting onto double-pointed needles. To do this, knit with the first double-pointed needle into the next stitch on the circular needle.

Continue to knit until about a third of your stitches are on the new needle. Make sure the stitches are not too close to the tips of the needle.

14 Take a second double-pointed needle and continue to work around the knitting until the next third of the stitches are on this needle. Knit the remaining stitches onto a third double-pointed needle.

15 Now you can keep knitting on your double-pointed needles using the fourth (empty) needle. Continue knitting until you have finished Round 55. You should have 32 stitches.

16 **Round 56:** From now on you need to decrease EVERY round as follows: starting with Round 56, knit six stitches, knit two stitches together and slip the stitch marker. Repeat this step three more times.

17 **Round 57:** Knit five stitches, knit two stitches together and

slip the stitch marker. Repeat this step three more times.

18 **Round 58:** Knit four stitches, knit two stitches together and slip the stitch marker. Repeat this step three more times.

19 **Round 59:** Knit three stitches, knit two stitches together and slip the stitch marker. Repeat this step three more times. You now have 16 stitches.

20 During this step, remove the stitch markers as you come to them. For Round 60 to the end: knit two stitches, knit two stitches together and then keep doing this until you have only four stitches left.

21 Put all the stitches onto one needle and knit them all together, pulling the end of the yarn through the stitches.

Earflaps

Find the beginning of your first round of knitting. This will be the centre back of your hat. Select the same colour yarn as you've got here to start the earflaps. You need to cast on by knitting into the cast-on edge of the hat.

Right-hand flap

▲ Put your needle through the 12th loop from the centre back point.

1 Count 12 cast-on loops from the centre back point. Hold the knitting with the reverse stocking side facing towards you. Put the tip of one of your 4mm needles through the 12th loop.

▲ Wrap the yarn around the needle and then knit it in the usual way.

2 Use your finger to wrap the yarn around the needle and then knit it in the usual way.

3 Continue to knit into cast-on loops, working away from the centre back until you have 23 stitches on your needle.

4 Now pick up your other needle and begin to work the 23 stitches as moss stitch. (Remember this? It means you need to knit one stitch, purl one stitch right to the end of the row.) Repeat this until you have six rows.

5 Change the colour of your yarn and repeat Step 4 until you have 12 rows of moss stitch.

6 Row 13: Purl two stitches together, then knit one, purl one all along the row until you reach the last two stitches. Purl these together.

7 Row 14: Knit two stitches together, then knit one, purl one all along the row until you reach the last two stitches. Knit these together.

8 Repeat Rows 13 and 14 until you have five stitches left (you'll be on Row 21). Then cast off and you've finished one ear.

Left-hand flap

You know how to do this now. Count 34 cast-on loops from the centre back point and put the tip of your needle through the 34th loop. Knit into cast-on loops, working towards the centre back until you have 23 stitches on your needle. Work in moss stitch as you did for the right-hand flap.

Finishing

Sew in and trim the ends inside the hat. There, you've finished!

▲ Trim the edge of the hat with blanket stitch.

Blanket stitch trim

In a contrasting colour yarn, blanket stitch all around the edge of the hat. This is a simple stitch that works well as an edging.

1 Thread a tapestry needle with a long strand of yarn.

2 Start by sewing in the end of the yarn about 1cm (½in) from the edge on the wrong side of your knitting.

3 Bring the threaded needle up around the edge of the knitting and stitch through from front to back about two rows in from the edge.

4 The next time you bring the needle up around the edge of the knitting, bring it through the loop of thread that you have just made.

5 Repeat from Step 3. This forms the blanket stitch.

Pompoms

Make three multicoloured pompoms following the instructions on page 16. Make them as big as you like but don't trim the tied ends yet.

Earflap pompoms

▲ Thread three strands of yarn through the bottom of the earflap.

1 Using a tapestry needle, thread three 20cm (8in) lengths of yarn halfway through the bottom point of an earflap.

▲ Braid the strands together and knot the end.

2 Braid the strands together for about 4cm (1½in) and then tie in a knot to secure.

3 Tie the ends of the braid securely to the ties on the pompom and trim the long ends.

4 Repeat Steps 1–3 for the other earflap pompom.

Top pompom

Using a tapestry needle, stitch the ties of the final pompom securely through the point at the top of the hat so that the pompom sits tightly on the hat. You did it! Your hat is now ready to wear!

Quick-knit mohair sweater

Knitting your first sweater will take less time than you think. Alternating odd-sized needles, one enormous and one chunky, means that the knitting grows like magic. Here, we stripe the mohair with another chunky yarn to make a lightweight yet cosy knit.

Remember to look at the pictures and instructions on pages 24–31, 54–57 and 70–71 whenever you need help with any of the techniques.

Warm and cuddly!

Sizes

Knitting patterns for clothing always include instructions for making different sizes. You could measure one of your favourite sweaters as a guide to which size will be right for you. It is better to make a sweater that is slightly too big than one that is too small. The instructions for the small size are given first, before the brackets. Inside the brackets, the first figure refers to the medium size. The second figure in the brackets is for the large size. To make following the pattern easier, you could circle all the instructions for your size with a pencil before you start knitting. The finished sizes for this sweater are as follows:
Small (medium, large)
Chest at underarm 88 (96, 104) cm or 35 (38, 41) inches
Length from shoulder 50 (56, 62) cm or 20 (22½, 25) inches
Sleeve length 35 (38, 41) cm or 14 (15, 16) inches

Back

Rib hem

1 Using 8mm knitting needles and the chunky yarn, cast on 46 (50, 54) stitches.

2 You need to work eight rows in double rib (you practised this in the Silly Sausages project on page 74).
Row 1: Knit two stitches. *Purl two stitches, knit two stitches.* Repeat the instructions between the asterisks to the end of the row.
Row 2: Purl two stitches. *Knit two stitches, purl two stitches.* Repeat the instructions between the asterisks to the end of the row.
Rows 3–8: Repeat Rows 1 and 2 three more times.

Mohair stripe

1 Swap the empty 8mm needle for a big 15mm needle. Using the mohair yarn, and with the big needle in your right hand, knit one row. Look at Knitting the Bracelet on pages 36 of the Rainbow Friendship Bands to remind yourself how to tie in a new yarn.

2 With the 8mm needle in your right hand, knit one row.

3 With the 15mm needle in your right hand, knit one row.

4 With the 8mm needle in your right hand, knit one row.

Chunky yarn stripe

1 Swap the empty 15mm needle for a 8mm needle. Now, going back to using the chunky yarn and 8mm needles in both hands, knit one row.

2 Purl one row. Knit one row. Purl one row.

Tension

Cast on 15 stitches using 8mm needles and knit a test piece, following the instructions for Mohair Stripe and Chunky Yarn Stripe. Work two stripes of each colour, then measure the tension (look back at page 92 if you've forgotten how). The tension for this sweater should be 10 stitches to 10cm (4in) and 16 rows to 12cm (4¾in). Count the stitches across a chunky yarn stripe. Count the rows down the whole test piece. If you have too many or too few stitches in your test piece, change the 8mm needles to a smaller or bigger size and knit another test piece. Keep the 15mm needle you use for the chunky yarn stripe the same for the moment. Keep changing the 8mm needles and knitting new test pieces until you get the right number of stitches. If you have too few rows at this stage, try changing the 15mm needle to a smaller one (you won't have the problem of too many rows).

Continuing the back

1 Repeat the stripe pattern in exactly the same way until you have 8 (9, 10) mohair stripes and 7 (8, 9) chunky yarn stripes.

2 Cast off all the stitches, using two 8mm needles. Be careful not to cast off the stitches too tightly.

Front

Make the front of the sweater in exactly the same way as the back until you have 7 (8, 9) mohair stripes and 6 (7, 8) chunky yarn stripes. Do not cast off because you have to shape the neck first.

Shaping the left side of the neck

1 When we refer to the left side of the neck, we mean the side that will be on the left when you're wearing the sweater. Change to the chunky yarn and both 8mm needles. Knit the first 16 (17, 19) stitches of the row.

2 Knit the next two stitches in the row together.

3 Slip the rest of the stitches onto a stitch holder. Look back at page 85 of Floppy Dollies to remind yourself how to do this. You can ignore these stitches until later. You now have 17 (18, 20) stitches left on the needle. Turn the work.

4 Purl the first two stitches together, then purl to the end of the row. You now have 16 (17, 19) stitches on the needle.

5 Knit the first 14 (15, 17) stitches, then knit the last two stitches together. You have 15 (16, 18) stitches on the needle.

6 Purl the first two stitches together, then purl to the end of the row. You have 14 (15, 17) stitches on the needle.

Continue adding stripes on the left side of the neck.

7 Change to the mohair yarn and, with the 15mm needle in your right hand, knit one row.

8 With the 8mm needle in your right hand, knit one row.

9 With the 15mm needle in your right hand, knit one row.

10 With the 8mm needle in your right hand, knit one row.

11 Cast off all 14 (15, 17) stitches using the 8mm needles.

Materials

- 220 (250, 280) metres or 240 (275, 310) yards of chunky yarn
- 120 (150, 180) metres or 135 (165, 200) yards of mohair yarn
- 8mm knitting needles
- One 15mm knitting needle
- 7mm knitting needles
- Stitch holder
- Scissors
- Tapestry needle
- 2 large towels
- Pins
- Tape measure
- Safety pins

Shaping the right side of the neck

1 When we refer to the right side of the neck, we mean the side that will be on the right when you're wearing the sweater. Slip the first 18 (19, 21) stitches onto a 8mm needle. Leave the remaining 10 (12, 12) stitches on the stitch holder. These stitches are at the centre front of the neck.

2 Rejoin the yarn. Using both 8mm needles and chunky yarn, knit the first two stitches together, then knit the remaining 16 (17, 19) stitches.

3 Purl the first 15 (16, 18) stitches, then purl the last two stitches together. You have 16 (17, 19) stitches on the needle.

4 Knit the first two stitches together, then knit to the end of the row. You have 15 (16, 18) stitches on the needle.

5 Purl the first 13 (14, 16) stitches, then purl the last two stitches together. You now have 14 (15, 17) stitches on the needle.

▲ Continue adding stripes on the right side of the neck.

6 Change to the mohair yarn and, with the 15mm needle in your right hand, knit one row.

7 With the 8mm needle in your right hand, knit one row.

8 With the 15mm needle in your right hand, knit one row.

9 With the 8mm needle in your right hand, knit one row.

10 Cast off all 14 (15, 17) stitches using the 8mm needles.

Sleeves

You need to knit two sleeves in exactly the same way.

Rib cuff

1 Using the 8mm needles and the chunky yarn, cast on 22 (26, 26) stitches.

2 You need to work eight rows in double rib.

Row 1: Knit two stitches. *Purl two stitches, knit two stitches.* Repeat the instructions between the asterisks to the end of the row.

Row 2: Purl two stitches. *Knit two stitches, purl two stitches.* Repeat the instructions between the asterisks to the end of the row.

3 Repeat these Rows 1 and 2 three more times.

More mohair stripes

1 You are now going to knit four rows in mohair yarn, just like you did for the back and front of the sweater. Swap the empty 8mm needle for the 15mm needle. Using the mohair yarn and, holding the big needle in your right hand, knit one row.

2 With the 8mm needle in your right hand, knit one row.

3 With the 15mm needle in your right hand, knit one row.

4 With the 8mm needle in your right hand, knit one row.

Chunky yarn stripe with increasing

The sleeves need to be shaped so that they become wider as you work up the arm. Swap the empty 15mm needle for a 8mm needle and change to the chunky yarn.

1 Knit one row, increasing at both ends of the row by knitting twice into the first stitch and then knitting twice into the last stitch (this is the bar increase method that you learned on page 55). You now have 24 (28, 28) stitches.

2 Purl all of the stitches on the next row of the sleeve.

3 Knit one row, increasing at both ends like you did in Step 1. You now have 26 (30, 30) stitches.

4 Purl all of the stitches on the next row of the sleeve.

Finishing the sleeve

1 Repeat the mohair and chunky yarn stripes, always increasing on the knit rows of the chunky yarn stripe, until you have 5 (5, 6) mohair stripes and 4 (4, 5) chunky yarn stripes. You should have 38 (42, 46) stitches on your needle.

2 Change to the chunky yarn and work 1 (2, 1) stripes without increasing any stitches. You should now have 10 (11, 12) stripes in total. The last stripe will be different for different sizes to get the correct sleeve length. The last stripe for the small size will be a chunky yarn stripe. The last stripe for the medium size will be a mohair stripe. The last stripe for the large size will be a chunky yarn stripe.

3 Cast off all the stitches. Now knit the second sleeve in the same way.

Assembling the sweater

Blocking

1 You need to make sure that all the pieces of your sweater are the right size before joining the seams. First, you will need to block the pieces just like you did with the Plaid Poncho on page 95. Do not pin out the ribs when blocking; let them relax into shape.

2 The back and front should be the same size: 44 (48, 52) cm or 17½ (19, 20½) inches wide and 50 (56, 62) cm or 20 (22½, 25) inches long. Both sleeves should be 35 (38, 41) cm or 14 (15, 16) inches long.

Right shoulder seam

1 Pin the front and back pieces together at the right shoulder seam, right sides facing.

2 Use mohair yarn and a small oversewing stitch to sew up the seam, like you did for the Funny-face Bag on page 34.

Neckband

▲ Mark the the position of the neck on the back piece of the sweater.

1 Lay the front piece of the sweater on top of the back piece. Use a stitch marker or safety pin to mark the place where the left side of the neck opening will be on the back piece. Don't pin the two pieces together.

▲ Pick up stitches to make the neckband.

2 Start making the neckband at the left shoulder on the front piece of knitting, with the right side of the knitting facing you. Use the chunky yarn and a 7mm knitting needle to pick up and knit twice into the first stitch. Look at Making the Neckband for the Plaid Poncho on page 96 to remind you how to do this. Pick up and knit nine more stitches down the left side of the neck.

3 Knit across the 10 (12, 12) stitches on the stitch holder at the centre front.

4 Pick up and knit ten stitches up the right front neck shaping.

5 Pick up and knit 17 (19, 19) stitches across the back piece of the sweater as far as the safety pin. Knit twice into the last stitch. You now have 50 (54, 54) stitches on the needle.

6 Pick up your second 7mm needle. Work four rows in double rib, starting with purl two stitches.

7 Cast off loosely. You have now finished the neckband.

Sewing the seams

1 Sew the left shoulder seam in the same way as you sewed the right.

2 Sew in all the loose ends to neaten the pieces before continuing.

Sewing sleeves in

1 Lay the sweater out, right side facing you, so that the shoulder seams are spread open. Fold a sleeve in half lengthways to find the centre and measure the width at the top.

△ Mark the position of the sleeves on the body of the sweater.

2 Measure this distance from the shoulder seam down the front and then down the back of the sweater. Use a safety pin or knot of yarn to mark this point at the edge of the fabric.

△ Sew the first sleeve in place.

3 With right sides together, lay the first sleeve in place, on the body, between the markers. Match the centre of the sleeve to the shoulder seam and pin in place.

4 Use a small oversewing stitch to join the seam. Repeat for the second sleeve on the other side of the sweater.

Mattress stitch

For the rest of the seams, you are going to use mattress stitch. This is really useful because it creates a seam that is invisible from the right side. It will also give you a really accurate way of matching the stripes.

1 Lay the pieces to be joined flat and edge to edge. The right side of the knitting should face upward.

2 Thread a tapestry needle with the chunky yarn and attach the yarn with a small stitch to the back of one piece of knitting.

△ Bring the needle to the front of the knitting between the first two stitches.

3 Sew through from the back to the front, bringing the needle out between the edge stitch and the second stitch in the first row.

△ Cross the needle over to the second piece of knitting.

4 Insert the needle between the edge stitch and the second stitch in the first row on the other piece of knitting. Pass the needle under the loop to the row above, then bring it back through to the front.

△ Now bring the needle back to the first piece of knitting.

5 Insert the needle into the hole that the stitch on the first side came out of. Pass it under the loop to the row above, even with the opposite side.

6 Repeat this process to make a zigzag between the edges. Make sure that you keep the sides even and do not miss any rows.

△ Pull the yarn gently to close up the seam after about five or six rows.

7 After about five or six rows, gently pull the yarn to close the seam, then continue sewing mattress stitch to the end of the seam.

8 Use mattress stitch to sew up the side seams, sleeves and the rib at the neck. Take your time so that you get a really neat result.

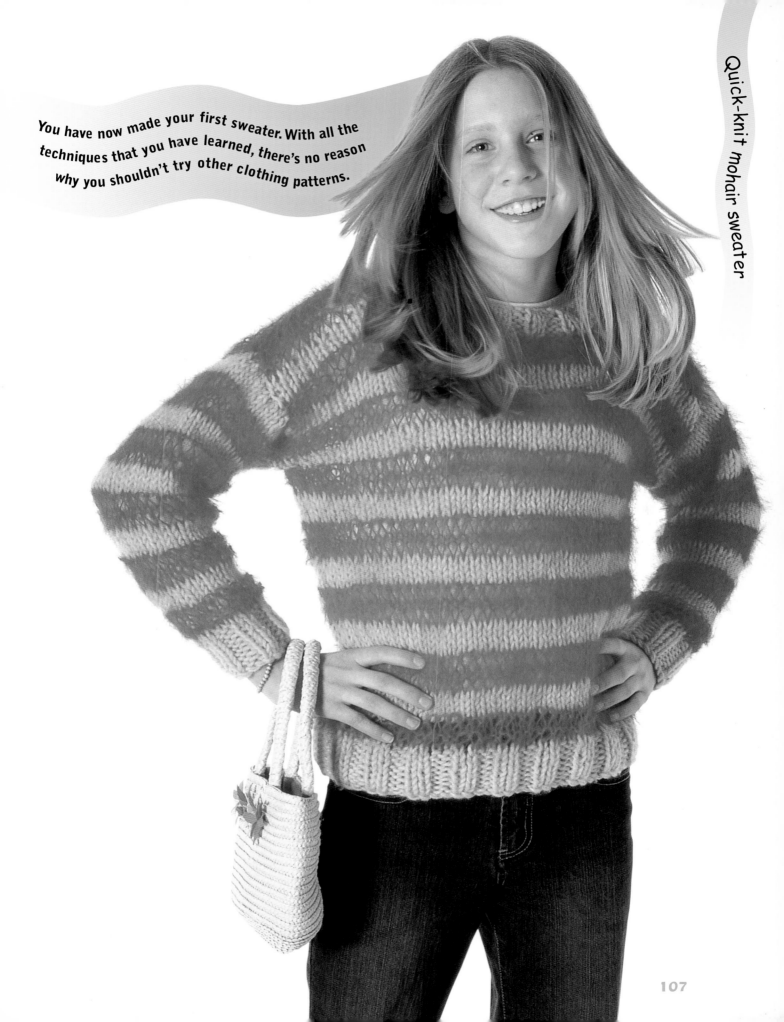

You have now made your first sweater. With all the techniques that you have learned, there's no reason why you shouldn't try other clothing patterns.

Help! I have no yarn

Don't worry. Whether you've knitted with every leftover piece of yarn that you can find or you want to try knitting with something different, you can make alternative 'yarns' by recycling outgrown clothes or plastic grocery bags. You can even knit with string and videotape. These 'yarns' are perfect for making unique rag rugs and rag bags.

Project 15

Making your own yarn

Making your own yarn is really easy, and by using it you will be able to knit things that are completely unique. Once you start looking around, you will realize that you have all that you need to make your first ball of yarn. Here are some ideas to get you started, but you will soon be coming up with your own.

Rag yarn

All you need to make yarn is a pair of scissors or pinking shears and lots of unwanted fabric. The easiest weight of fabric to start with is that of worn-out or outgrown clothes, such as shirts or T-shirts. You could also try old sheets, pillowcases, duvets, curtains, tablecloths or fabric remnants from a sewing shop.

▲ Cut any clothing along the seams and lay the pieces flat.

1 First of all, cut any clothing apart along the seams so that the pieces lie more or less flat.

▲ Look closely at woven fabric to see where the straight grain is.

2 Look closely at the fabric. Woven fabrics, such as linen and cotton,

are made up of straight lines of threads that have been woven together. Half the lines will go up and down, and the other half weave in and out of them from side to side. These straight lines are called the 'straight grain' of the fabric.

▲ Cut or tear woven fabric into strips.

3 Cut or tear a straight line along the edge of the woven fabric, following the straight grain. Most woven fabrics will tear straight along the grain if you make a small snip at the edge of the fabric first.

Let it rip!

▲ Tear the strips if you want a frayed edge.

4 If you tear the strips, the yarn you are making will have a nice frayed edge.

▲ Use pinking shears to cut strips with a zigzag edge.

5 Try cutting the fabric with pinking shears if you want to make yarn with a zigzag edge.

▲ Cut up jersey fabric with scissors to make yarn with a rolled edge.

6 It is usually better to cut rather than tear jersey fabrics, like T-shirts. These will make yarn with a rolled edge.

▲ Pull the strips gently to make sure they are strong enough.

7 Decide how wide you want the yarn to be. A strip that is about 1–2cm (¼–¾in) wide is suitable for most fabrics. Do not cut heavier fabrics, like denim, too wide or the yarn will be too bulky to knit. Gently pull both ends of the first strip you cut to make sure it does not fall apart. If it is too weak, try cutting a little wider for the rest of the strips.

8 Now simply cut or tear lots of strips in the same way.

▲ Tie the strips together and roll them up into a ball.

9 To make your strips into yarn, tie the ends together to make a long length. You could mix lots of different colours together and make one huge, multicoloured ball of yarn, or divide them into several balls of separate colours for knitting stripes. As you tie the strips together, roll the yarn you are making into a ball so that it doesn't get tangled.

Rag yarn is ideal for making rugs and bags (see pages 114–119), or even for making funny-looking juggling balls. Always check with an adult before you start cutting things up, though!

Plastic bag yarn

This yarn is great for making a waterproof mat or a useful swim bag. This time you just need your scissors and lots of plastic bags.

▲ Cut each bag open and lay it flat.

1 Cut the sides of the bags open so that they lie flat. Cut off any handles.

2 Cut a straight line along the edge of the bag, then fold 2–4cm (¾–1½in) of the plastic over the blade of the scissors at the edge you have just cut. It is best to fold over a narrow strip of plastic if you are using thick bags, or a wider strip if you are using thin, lightweight bags.

▲ Slide a pair of scissors along the fold to cut a strip of plastic.

3 Pinch the folded bag firmly between the fingers of one hand, then use your other hand to slide the scissors along the fold, cutting the plastic. This is a quick way to slice the plastic into strips. Keep the bag taut as you cut.

4 Tie the plastic strips together to make balls of yarn, like you did for the rag yarn.

Other types of yarn

When you think about it, you will soon realize that you can knit with any long, flexible strip or thread. Here are some more yarn ideas that you may like to try for fun. Just ask permission before you start knitting.

● **String** or **garden twine** is a cheap alternative to conventional yarn and is already in a ball. It knits into a strong, open fabric.

● **Raffia** is good for knitting a natural-style beach bag or mat.

● **Fishing line** is great for creating invisible knitting, so try putting an invisible stripe into your work.

Recycling yarn

A traditional method of reusing yarn is to unravel unwanted knitted garments. Use a small pair of scissors to pick seams apart and cut the cast-off stitches at the top of the knitting. The fabric will unravel surprisingly quickly. Ball up each length of yarn as you go. This recycled yarn is great for knitting small toys and dolls' clothes, or knit lots of squares to make a patchwork blanket.

Different fabrics will make different types of yarn. You can even make a really springy, lightweight yarn from stockings and pantyhose that have runs!

● **Fine-gauge wire**, such as fuse wire, knits into a wonderful, flexible fabric that you can mould into different shapes. Try making mini sculptures or a spectacular metal version of one of the Fantastic Flowers on pages 42–47. You will need to fold in the ends of the wire carefully so that they don't catch on your clothes or other fabrics.

● **Videotape, clothesline, shoelaces** ... the list is almost endless.

● **Ribbons** and **braid** can be used to make an attractive trim for other pieces of knitting. Just knit a few rows with it, then stitch it in place.

Now you will never run out of yarn. Just be inventive and you can always keep knitting.

Rag rug and bag

A new lease of life for old shirts and dresses, this rug is suitable for the bathroom or bedroom, or as a sleeping mat for a favourite pet. Try the same thing with recycled plastic bags and you will have a waterproof picnic blanket. You could even fold a rag-knitted rectangle in half and add handles to make a strong, unique bag that will last forever.

These projects are really easy. To make the yarn, look back at the instructions on pages 110–113, then use the basic knitting skills you learned on pages 24–31.

Rag rug

It is difficult to specify the quantity of yarn needed for this project, because every rag yarn is a bit different. However, as a guide, our rag rug used about 600g (1¼ pounds) of light- to medium-weight cotton fabrics that had been cut into strips 2cm (¾in) wide. You could weigh your yarn on a kitchen scale to check that you have enough, but it's easy to make more if you need to.

Knotty knitting!

Materials

● About 400g (14oz) of rag yarn in the main colour

● About 200g (7oz) of rag yarn in the second colour

● Several small balls of rag yarn in contrasting colours

● 15mm knitting needles

● Scissors

Save some of the cast-on yarn to use at the bottom edge of the rug before you cast off, so that both ends behave in the same way.

Starting the rug

1 Cast on 30–40 stitches in the main colour. Cast on in the usual way, keeping the stitches quite loose, so that you will be able to knit into them easily. If they are too close together on the needle, you will find knitting difficult.

2 Now, working in knit stitch, complete the first row. Knit loosely, so that the stitches can slide along the needles easily. When you come to a knot in the yarn, just keep knitting

and the ends of the knot will become part of the fabric design.

3 At the end of the row, simply turn the knitting and continue in knit stitch as you would when knitting with ordinary yarn. You need to knit a total of six rows of the main colour, and then you can start adding stripes.

Knitting stripes

▲ Tie on a new colour at the start of a row and keep knitting.

1 To change colour at the end of a row, cut the yarn, leaving a short tail. Tie on the second colour so that the knot sits by the needle, and start knitting the next row in the new yarn.

2 Knit the next two rows in the second colour.

3 Repeat Steps 1–2 to add lots more colourful stripes to your rug. It will look good if you knit a stripe for just a single row now and then (in other words, just do Step 1).

▲ Pause halfway along a row and stretch out your knitting to check what the pattern looks like.

4 As you knit, you will start to get a good idea of how far your yarn goes. This will make it easier to plan your stripe pattern. If you pause halfway across a row, you can stretch out the width of the rug more easily and look at the stripes.

5 When your rug is almost as long as you wish, change back to the main colour and knit a few rows. When you are happy with the length and look of your rug, you need to cast off. Do this in the usual way, but be very careful not to cast off tightly, because this will gather in one end of the rug so that it is narrower than the rest.

Finishing the rug

Lay the rug out flat and trim any ends that you think are too long. The random knots are part of the design of a rag rug. If you want even more knots, you can cut some short lengths of rag yarn and tie them into the knitting wherever you like.

Next you could try knitting a plastic bag rug to use as a mat for sitting on outdoors. Use smaller needles – 10mm would be good.

Rag bag

This bag has been knitted with multicoloured rag yarn, made by knotting together random strips of different light- to medium-weight fabrics. The strips were cut about 1.5cm (½in) wide.

Materials

- About 200g (7oz) of multicoloured rag yarn
- Ball of string
- 10mm knitting needles
- Scissors
- Large tapestry needle

Starting the bag

1 Cast on 30 stitches using the multicoloured rag yarn.

2 Work the first four rows in knit stitch.

3 Cut the yarn, leaving a short tail. Tightly tie on the end of a ball of string, with the knot close to the needle. Knit six rows in string.

4 Cut the string, leaving a short tail, and tie on the rag yarn once again. Knit four rows in rag yarn.

▲ Continue alternating stripes of rag yarn and string.

5 Continue striping the string and rag yarn until the knitting is twice as long as you want your finished bag to be. Finish with four rows of rag yarn and cast off.

Sewing up the bag

1 Fold the knitting in half to make the bag shape. Make sure the cast-on and cast-off edges meet at the top.

▲ Tie a length of string to the top two corners on one side of the bag.

2 Cut a 60cm (24in) length of string and tie the end securely through the cast-on and cast-off stitches at the top of the bag, on one side. Thread the string onto a large tapestry needle.

▲ Oversew the seams securely.

3 Use an oversewing stitch to join the seam securely, sewing into each stitch at the edge of the bag, like you did on page 34 of the Funny-face Bag. Sew a few stitches one on top of the other to secure the end.

4 Sew the end of the string into the knitting and tie to the nearest knot in the yarn.

5 Repeat Steps 2–4 on the other side of the bag.

Knotty knitting!

Making handles

1 Cut six lengths of rag yarn about 50cm (20in) long each.

2 Tie them all together at one end, leaving tails 5cm (2in) long.

▲ Braid the yarn and knot the ends securely.

3 Divide the lengths of yarn into three bunches (there'll be two pieces of yarn in each bunch). Braid the bunches of yarn for 35cm (14in). If you need a reminder, you learned braiding on page 17. Knot the end of the braid to secure it.

▲ Thread the handle through the top row of string.

4 Thread both ends of the braid through the top edge of one side of the bag to make a handle. Thread it through the top row of string from the outside of the bag to the inside. The handle should be in the centre of the edge, and the ends should be threaded through about 10cm (4in) apart.

▲ Sew the ends of the braid into the middle and knot them together.

5 Sew each end in and out of the stitches, working towards the centre of the bag, and tie them together on the wrong side of the fabric so that the ends of the braid join to form a strong handle. Trim the ends of the braid.

▲ Tie a strip of yarn around each end of the handle to strengthen it.

6 Tie a 10cm (4in) length of rag yarn through the top row of knitting and around the handle on each side, to hold it in place. Trim the ends.

7 Repeat Steps 1–6 to make a second handle, and your bag is ready to go.

117

Project 16

Lining the bag

The bag is great for carrying things like groceries, schoolbooks, a football or balls of yarn, but if you want to carry smaller items, like knitting needles or pencils, you will need to sew lining inside to keep things from falling out.

Materials

- Piece of fabric to fit inside bag (see Step 1 below)

- - - - - - - - - - - - - -

- Pins

- - - - - - - - - - - - - -

- Sewing thread and needle

- - - - - - - - - - - - - -

- Scissors

▲ Figure out the size of fabric you will need to fit inside the bag.

1 Measure the width of your bag and add 3cm (1in); write this number down. Measure the length of your bag, multiply it by 2, then add 4cm (1½in); write this number down. Lay out the piece of fabric and measure the width and length you have written down. Cut out the fabric to this size.

2 Fold the fabric in half, right sides together, and pin the edges.

3 Thread the sewing needle and knot both ends together to double the thread. Backstitch the seam, like you did on page 76 of the Silly Sausages project, 1.5cm (½in) in from the edge. Keep the stitches quite small and neat. This will make a strong seam.

▲ Backstitch both seams.

4 Repeat Step 3 for the other seam, then remove the pins.

▲ Fold over the top edge and pin in place.

5 Fold the top edge over 2cm (¾in) to the wrong side. Pin from the right side to hold the fold in place.

6 Place the lining inside the bag so that the folded top edge is 2cm (¾in) below the top of the bag. Use a few more pins to hold the fabric in place.

▲ Oversew the top of the lining to the bag.

7 Oversew the lining into the bag, stitching over the edge of the fold and into the rag yarn all the way around the top of the lining.

8 Remove the pins and your lining is complete.

Rag yarn is ideal for making unique knitted items. Why not try making a smaller version of the bag with longer straps to use as a shoulder bag?

Knotty knitting!

Now all you have to do is decide what to keep in your new bag. The instructions will produce a bag that is just the right size to store your knitting equipment and knitting projects.

Oh, no! What went wrong?

When learning any new skill, you are bound to find that some things don't turn out as planned. The first thing to remember is DON'T PANIC. Even the most experienced knitters occasionally make a mistake. With time and practice, you will learn that it is always easier to correct any problems as soon as you spot them.

Getting help

A problem often seems much smaller if somebody can help you with it. If you need guidance, ask another knitter for advice. If somebody in your household can knit, that person may be able to help. Find out if any of your teachers knit. You will probably find lots of willing advice at your local yarn or craft shop. If you can't find anybody to help you, look at this list of common problems and you may find a solution. Also re-read the instructions in the projects to make sure that you are following them correctly.

Oh, no! My knitting looks uneven

Tension the yarn

It takes practice to get the tension of the yarn even. Review Holding the Yarn on page 27 and remind yourself how to tension the yarn with your fingers. You may find that you can add tension by holding the working end of the yarn between your knees or running it over your shoulder.

Reposition your stitches

While you are knitting, try to keep the stitches towards the tips of the needles so that they don't get too stretched.

Finish the row

Finish a row before stopping your knitting, because stitches get stretched and may even get dropped if you stop halfway.

Wash it

Washing a garment or piece of knitting will often help to even up the stitches. Follow the instructions on the ball band and in Caring for Your Knitting on page 125 to see how to do this.

Oh, no! My knitting is the wrong size

Check the tension

If your knitting is the wrong size, the first thing to do is to check the tension. Refer to page 92 to review the information about tension. Always make a test piece before starting a garment or it may not fit.

Keep count

You may have cast on too many or too few stitches, or knitted the wrong number of rows, so check the pattern. It is a good idea to use a pencil and paper to count the rows as you knit them, and also to check, now and again, that you have the right number of stitches in a row. If you are using a pattern that has different sizes, make sure that you have circled all the instructions for the size you are knitting.

Oh, no! There are too many stitches in the row

Check the position of your yarn

Your yarn may be in the wrong place at the beginning or in the middle of a row. When you are about to do a knit stitch, the yarn should be behind the needle before you make the stitch. When you are about to do a purl stitch, the yarn should be in front of the needle before you make the stitch. If the yarn is in the wrong place, you will create an extra loop that will look like a stitch – this is like accidentally making a yarnover. You will be able to see a little hole in the row where you made the mistake.

Check your stitch technique

You may have knitted twice into a stitch, like increasing. Make sure you always slip the stitch off the left needle before working into the next stitch. Make sure you are knitting only into the stitch on the left needle and not knitting into the strand between two stitches.

Pick up the whole stitch

You may have split a stitch into two and worked into it twice. This can happen with loosely twisted or very textured yarns, or when you are knitting two ends of yarn together. Be very careful to pick up the whole stitch and not to push the needle through the middle of the yarn.

Oh, no! There aren't enough stitches in the row

Knit one stitch at a time

You may have accidentally knitted two stitches together, like decreasing. Make sure that you knit into only one stitch at a time. Use your fingertip to spread apart the stitches at the tip of the left needle if they are sitting very close together.

Look for a dropped stitch

You may have dropped a stitch, so refer to Oh, No! I've Dropped a Stitch (see right).

Oh, no! I've dropped a stitch

Pick it up again

Slightly different techniques are used to pick up stitches, depending on what stitch pattern you knit. You learned how to pick up a dropped garter stitch on page 49 of the Supersize Scarf. The methods of picking up both knit and purl stocking stitches are explained in the Cosmic Clutch Bag on page 80. You can see how to mend a stocking stitch ladder in the Plaid Poncho on pages 94–95. If you get a ladder when you are working in garter stitch, count the number of strands in the ladder. If there is an even number, start at Step 1 below. If there is an odd number, start at Step 3.

Even number of strands

1 Push a crochet hook through the loop at the bottom of the ladder, from front to back, and then catch the strand above the loop in the hook.

2 Pull the strand through the stitch on the hook. The strand has now become a new stitch. Carefully remove the hook from the stitch. If you now have an odd number of strands, continue with Step 3. If you have reached the top of the ladder, go to Step 5.

Odd number of strands

3 Push a crochet hook through the loop at the bottom of the ladder, from back to front, and then catch the strand above the loop in the hook.

4 Pull the strand through the stitch on the hook to make a new stitch. You will now have an even number of strands in the ladder (unless you have reached the top). Carefully remove the hook from the stitch.

5 Alternate the instructions for even and odd numbers of strands until all the strands have been made into stitches. Lift the last stitch onto the left needle, making sure that it doesn't get twisted, and continue to work the row.

Oh, no! My cast-on and cast-off are too tight . . . or too loose

Undo the knitting

Examine the cast-on after you have knitted a few rows. If it looks wrong, undo the knitting and start again because you will not be able to correct this when the knitting is finished. The cast-on row needs to be a bit stretchy, like the knitting. If it is too tight, it will pull the knitting in. Check the cast-off after the first few stitches so that you do not have to unravel the whole row and do it again.

Use bigger or smaller needles

If your cast-on is too tight, try using a needle one size bigger than the knitting for the first row, then change to the recommended size needle for the rest of the pattern. If the cast-on is too loose, try using a needle one size smaller for the cast-on row. This is important if you are knitting a springy rib to pull in at the edge of a sweater. Lots of patterns recommend using smaller sized needles for all the rib trims on a garment. If the cast-off is too tight, you can try changing to a needle one size bigger for the cast-off row. You may have problems getting a sweater over your head if the cast-off is too tight. If the cast-off is too loose and pulls the knitting out, try using a smaller needle for the cast-off row to make it tighter.

Oh, no! My yarn is running out

Start a new ball

Each row of knitting uses a piece of yarn about three times the width of the knitting. If you do not have a length of yarn that measures about four times the width of the knitting, change to a new ball so that you will have plenty of yarn to complete the row.

Buy an extra ball

It is always better to buy an extra ball of yarn before you start making something, even though most patterns build in an extra amount. You can always use spare yarn on a smaller project. Most shops will gladly give a refund or shop credit for unused balls of yarn if you provide a receipt. However, it's always best to ask about shop policy before you buy.

Buy matching yarn

If you do need to buy more yarn after you've started a project, you will need to match the shade number and dye lot of your original yarn. Look at the ball band of the previous ball and check the details, as listed in Ball Band Information on page 9. Go back to the shop where you bought the yarn and see if it has any in stock – you may be lucky. It is not a good idea to change to a different dye lot in the middle of a single-colour piece of knitting because it will show up as a stripe. If you really have no choice, try knitting the new colour where it will be less obvious; for example, on the trim or for a whole section.

Oh, no! I can't find the right yarn

Check the ball band

Most patterns suggest a suitable weight of yarn to use. If the pattern has to be a certain size, like a sweater, it is important to find a yarn that knits to the correct tension – look at Ball Band Information on page 9 and Measuring Tension on page 92. Sometimes it won't matter if the knitting comes out a bit smaller or bigger; for example, a bag or a scarf. In this case, look at the ball bands on a number of yarns to find one that has a similar weight and see which needles are recommended.

Oh, no! I need to unravel some of my knitting

Ask for help or start again

Unravelling rows of knitting is quite difficult for a beginner, so if somebody offers to help you, always say 'Yes, please' with a big smile. If you have knitted only a few rows when you spot a mistake, it may be quicker and easier to start the whole piece again.

Unravel stitch by stitch

If the mistake is on the same row on which you are currently working, unravel your knitting stitch by stitch to right before the mistake.

1 On a knit row, insert the tip of the left-hand needle, from front to back, into the stitch immediately below the first stitch on the right-hand needle. Slip the stitch onto the left needle.

2 Gently pull the working end of the yarn to undo the stitch above the one you slipped onto the left needle. Continue in this way until you have reached the stitch before you made the mistake.

3 On a purl row, insert the tip of the left-hand needle, from front to back, into the stitch immediately below the first stitch on the right-hand needle. Slip the stitch onto the left needle.

4 Gently pull the working end of the yarn to undo the stitch above the one you slipped onto the left needle. Continue in this way until you have reached the stitch before you made the mistake.

Unravel row by row

If the mistake is on a previous row, unravel your knitting row by row back to before you made the mistake. Be patient and don't try to rush. If you have been making a note of the number of rows you have knitted as part of your pattern, don't forget to count how many rows you unravel so that you know where you are in the pattern after you have finished unravelling.

1 Find a knitting needle that is thinner than the one you were knitting with.

2 Lay the knitting on a flat, clean surface. Slide the stitches off the needle and pull the yarn gently to unravel the knitting and leave the row with the mistake at the top of the knitting. Do this slowly and very carefully.

3 Lay the knitting sideways so that the working end of the yarn appears from the bottom right-hand corner. Insert the tip of the thinner needle into the stitch below the first unraveled loop, pointing towards the other end of the row and coming from the back to the front of the stitch.

4 Gently pull the end of the yarn to unravel the loop as far as the next stitch.

5 Pick up the stitches one at a time along the row in this way, unravelling the wrong row as you go. You will end up with all the stitches on the thinner needle. Breathe a sigh of relief – you have saved your knitting. Well done.

6 Now, using one of the correct size needles, work the next row. Make sure that you continue the pattern from the right place.

7 Put down the thinner needle and continue with the pattern using both correct needles.

Caring for your knitting

You have put a lot of effort into making your own hand-knitted things, so you will want to keep them looking good and make them last a long time.

Washing

Some yarns, especially synthetic fibres, can be machine washed. Other yarns, like wool, need to be washed by hand. Follow the washing instructions on the yarn's ball band. If you lose the band or are not sure how to wash your yarn, always hand wash in lukewarm water.

Hand washing

1 Dissolve some mild detergent recommended for your fibres in lukewarm water. Gently squeeze the knitting in the soapy water to loosen the dirt. Do not rub the fabric. Leave the knitting in the water for about five minutes.

2 Let the water drain away, then gently squeeze out as much water as you can. Add fresh lukewarm water and squeeze the knitting to rinse away the suds. Drain the water and repeat until the water is clear.

3 Gently squeeze out the water and then lay the garment flat on a thick, dry, colourfast towel. Roll up the towel with the knitting inside and press down on the roll to help the towel absorb most of the water.

4 Lay out another dry towel, away from direct sunlight or heat sources like radiators, and put the garment on it. The garment should be laid flat and pulled into its usual shape and size. Leave it like this until completely dry.

Machine washing

Stick to the recommended temperature on the yarn's ball band and use the gentlest setting possible. You can place the garment inside a pillowcase before putting it in the machine to prevent it from stretching. Take the knitted piece out of the machine as soon as the cycle has finished. Dry the garment by following Step 4 of Hand Washing. If you are unsure about the washing instructions, or do not have permission or help to use a machine, hand wash instead.

Storing

Do not put your knitting on a hanger because it will stretch and pull out of shape. Instead, fold knitted items and store them in a drawer or on a shelf. If your knitting is to be stored for a long time, make sure it is clean before you put it away. Moths love to spoil woollen garments by stealing fibres to make their cocoons. You can protect the garments from moths by using a natural moth repellent such as cedar chips. Try to keep stored knits sealed in a plastic bag or shake them out in the daylight regularly.

Washing Symbols

40°C 104°F — Machine washable at the maximum water temperature shown in the symbol

Hand wash only

Hot iron

Warm iron

Cool iron

Can be treated with bleach

Can be tumble dried

Dry cleanable

A large cross through any of the symbols means that you should not use that process on your yarn – for example, a cross through a symbol of an iron means 'Do not iron'.

Understanding patterns

The projects in this book have been explained clearly in a step-by-step way so that a beginner can easily follow them. If you have ever looked at the instructions in other knitting patterns, you may have noticed that they are written very differently.

Don't be put off

Knitting patterns are usually written without full sentences and use lots of strange words that you probably won't recognize. These odd-looking words are just abbreviations for the same knitting instructions you've been using in this book. Following a pattern is usually quite easy because everything is written in the right order and uses more or less the same terms and abbreviations. Some patterns include an alphabetical list of abbreviations and an explanation of what they all mean, but knitters soon learn the most commonly used ones. If you do see an abbreviation that is not on the list shown here, check the information on the pattern to see if it is explained or ask a more experienced knitter to help you translate.

Example

With a bit of practice, you will find that reading patterns comes easily to you. Start by looking at this set of instructions and guess what you would have knitted (the answer is on page 128).

Sizes: small (medium, large)
Cast on 10 sts using 5mm needles and double-knitting cotton yarn.
Row 1. K to end.
Rep this row 5 more times.
*Row 7. (k2tog.) Rep to end of row.
Row 8. K to end.
Rep this row 7 more times.
Row 16. (kfb) rep to end of row.
Row 17. K to end.
Rep this row 5 more times.
Rep from * 4 (5,6) more times.
Cast off all sts.

Common abbreviations

alt	alternate
beg	beginning
CC	contrast colour
col	colour
cm	centimetres
cont	continue
dec	decrease/decreasing
dpn	double-pointed needles
foll	following
g, gr or gm	grams
G st	garter stitch
in	inches
inc	increase/increasing
k	knit
kfb	knit into front and back of stitch (increasing)
k2tog	knit 2 together
LH	left hand
lp	loop
meas	measures
m	metres
MC	main colour
oz	ounce(s)
p	purl
pat(t)	pattern
psso	pass slip stitch(es) over
rem	remaining
rep	repeat
RH	right hand
rib	ribbing
rnds or rds	rounds
RS	right side
sl	slip
sl st	slip stitch
st(s)	stitch(es)
st st	stocking stitch
tbl	through back of loop
tog	together
WS	wrong side
wyib	with yarn in back
wyif	with yarn in front
yd(s)	yard(s)
yo	yarn over needle (to make extra stitch)
"	inches
* or ( )	asterisks or brackets are used to show a set of instructions that need to be repeated a stated number of times

Index

Credits

Quarto would like to thank Ashley Beattie, Ryan Harris, Arabel Jordan, Charlotte Knight, Hettie
Reatchlous, Tattie Reatchlous, Alex Sesiuk, Jack Sesiuk, Freya Tomley and Milly Wright for
modelling the projects in this book. All photographs and illustrations are the copyright of Quarto.

Author's acknowledgements
Thanks to my lovely knitting mum Helen Clewer for lots of help and inspiration, and to
Tiphaine de Lussy, Rachel Cattle, Alison Cooke and Zena Barrie for being such enthusiastic
knitters and pompom makers!

Answer to knitting pattern example on page 126: You would have knitted the Desert Island Belt project from pages 62–65.